# THE CREATIVE K-1 CLASSROOM

## MAKING AND MANAGING A PLAYFUL LEARNING ENVIRONMENT

WRITTEN BY CHERYL APGAR

EDITOR: KRISTINE JOHNSON

ILLUSTRATOR: DARCY TOM

DESIGNER: MOONHEE PAK

CONTRIBUTING EDITOR: WENDY BLOCHER

PROJECT DIRECTOR: CAROLEA WILLIAMS

# Table of Contents

Even without all of the research, each of us intuitively knows how we learn best. Some of us prefer reading information from a book. Others prefer listening to a speaker. Some need pictures and charts. Others need to touch. Most of us use multiple learning modalities, and students do, too. Research reinforces that these are all valid ways of learning.

But what about the children? All it seems they want to do is play. Teachers know how difficult it is for children to sit still. Let's face it, kids are kids. They want to talk and move around. They want to laugh and have a good time.

Can we capitalize on this concept in education? Absolutely! And if we do, we will have students who can hardly wait to come to school each day—students who will be excited about learning and actively involved in the learning process because play, by its very nature, is fun. Students enjoy and look forward to even the most challenging skills and concepts because of the expectation of fun. When we make learning playful, learning becomes the end result of having a good time. *The Creative K–1 Classroom* maximizes instructional effectiveness by allowing children to be children. The teaching tips and instructional strategies in this resource will help you move your students from the traditional "drill and kill" to "yearn to learn." And when students yearn to learn, miracles happen.

*The Creative K–1 Classroom* helps you create an environment where learning happens. In this book, you will discover ways to meet your state and district curriculum standards while using your time in an efficient manner to maximize the learning in every moment of the school day. As you incorporate the suggestions for learning and discovery centers, students will learn to become independent thinkers and workers, allowing you more time to work with individuals and small groups to meet specific learning objectives. *The Creative K–1 Classroom* provides an avenue to make it happen.

# GETTING ORGANIZED

Develop a plan of action to efficiently meet

specific goals and objectives. Establish classroom policies to

carry you through the year. Highly effective teachers know where they

are going and how they are going to get there. The following are some sug-

gestions to help you become more

effective by being more

efficient.

## Student Questionnaire

Send home the Student Questionnaire (page 7)

at Back-to-School Night. Ask parents to fill it out with their

child. This provides valuable insight into the lives of your students

and gives parents an opportunity to bring up sensitive subjects that

might be important to a child's success. Be sure to keep the informa-

tion confidential. The information should help you better understand

a child's circumstances and be sensitive to his or her needs. Also,

the questionnaire can help you be aware of special interests

or family celebrations and traditions to incorporate

into your curriculum.

## Unit Planner

Plan each lesson to include a broad variety of instructional strategies. Use the Unit Planner (page 8) to ensure all the parts of the curriculum are included. Refer to and add to this planner each year to simplify your future planning and ensure a fully integrated curriculum.

## School Calendar

Start the year with a calendar for the entire year. Write each week of the school year above each box on the School Calendar (page 9). Schedule the "have-tos" and other programs already determined by the master school calendar. Fill in your curriculum, themes, and units of study around the seasons and school holidays. To help plan your curriculum around themes and topics you want to cover, write out the months of the year and record the topics or themes around the seasons. If your curriculum focuses on certain letters or literature, have your topics complement them.

## Supplies

Avoid the "Gimme, gimme. That's mine!" syndrome by making all classroom materials community property. Keep crayons, glue, pencils, and scissors on tables in tote containers with a handle. Extras can be kept in a cabinet for replacement as needed. Provide a separate container for pencils needing sharpening. This eliminates the need for students to get up and sharpen a pencil during class. Simply have a volunteer sharpen pencils before or after school.

## Teacher's Basket

Have a special place for students to place their work and messages to you. The morning "Teacher, Teacher . . ." is eliminated if students know exactly where to put things that require your attention. If you place a basket outside the door, you can train students to get into the routine of turning in their work before going out to play. It also allows parents to deposit notes without coming into the classroom—especially when students are tardy.

### Cubbies

So many things need to be distributed each day. It can waste valuable instructional time to pass things out to students individually. Instead, eliminate clutter, noise, and wasted minutes by placing a set of cubbies at the back of the room. Place a box or basket labeled *To Be Delivered* next to the cubbies. Lay everything there that needs to go home. During the day, assign a parent volunteer or student to "deliver the mail."

### Folders

Eliminate the "trashed" look of papers that tend to be stuffed into desks and backpacks by giving each student a special "School Folder." Teach students to be responsible and to care for their homework, notes, and papers. As they enter the room, have students empty the contents of their folder into a teacher's basket and place the folder in their cubby. At the end of each day, have students place all "cubby stuff" neatly into their folder to take home. Ask parents to check the folder daily for important information and review their child's activities. Attach homework and home-reading records to the folders as needed.

### Newsletters

Regular communication with parents is an important tool for establishing a strong home–school connection. A weekly newsletter is not only good PR, it eliminates the "Nobody told me!" syndrome and gives you an opportunity to inform parents about your class's activities and needs. Record on the Newsletter (page 10) what students studied the week before, what they will study the current week, and what they will cover the following week. Include all curricular 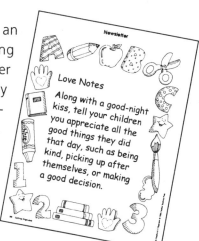 areas, important dates, and the "student spotlight" (see page 99), or student of the week. Provide reminders about special events such as field trips, picture day, assemblies, or holidays. Give special thanks to volunteers or helpers. Advertise requests for drivers, helpers, or volunteers to help with special projects or outings. As space allows, highlight student work and comments. For a sweet touch, add a special "Love Notes" section to give parents ideas for showing love to their children. For example, suggest that parents write a love note and place it in their child's lunch box.

### Love Notes

Write suggested ways for parents to show their love to their children, and send home these little "love notes." The book *101 Ways to Tell Your Child "I Love You"* by Vicki Lansky has some great ideas. Suggest the book, or make up some of your own love notes. Write them on your weekly newsletter. Parents will appreciate receiving creative ways to share their love, and their child will reflect the love spread at home.

# Student Questionnaire

Child's Name _____     Mother's Name _____

Father's Name _____     Parents' Professions _____

What do you feel are your child's strengths?

_____

Weaknesses?

_____

What special interests does your child have outside of school?

_____

Does your child have an allergy or a physical or medical situation of which I need to be aware?

_____

What celebrations, traditions, and holidays do you share as a family?

_____

Is there anything you would like to share about your family history?

_____

Do you have any special interests or hobbies you could share with our class?

_____

What is important to your child?

_____

What would you like me to know about your child?

_____

Have your child help complete this sentence: I hope my teacher . . .

_____

# Unit Planner

| | | | |
|---|---|---|---|
| Writing | Math Center | ABC Center | |

| Cooking | Music | Think and Do Center | Literacy Center |

| Art | P.E. | Unit | Computers | Bulletin Boards | Visitors/Field Trips |

| Activities | Stories | Poetry |

| Concepts and Vocabulary | Reading Program | Social Studies | Math | Science |

# School Calendar

# Newsletter

# SETTING THE TONE

The tone you set for the class influences the effectiveness of learning and affects every interaction between you and your students. It is the teacher who sets the mood, so start the year out right by demonstrating kindness and love in all that you do. Set the mood each day by having the class recite songs, poems, chants, and affirmations that reinforce classroom standards and personal worth. Class-spirit chants and songs build a sense of community and develop oral-language proficiency. Have students follow along with songs and chants written on chart paper to promote print-awareness. Add actions to enhance coordination and the development of rhythm. You will find students modify their behavior and support their friends in a more positive way when they have been taught and reminded what to do and say. Use these unique and fun ideas to set a positive tone for the year.

## Spirit Cheer

**MATERIALS**

"We've Got the Spirit" cheer

Invite students to read the cheer below and make up motions to go with it.

**We've Got the Spirit**
The kids in room _____
Just can't be beat.
We've got the spirit
Clear down in our feet.
We like to learn,
To read and write . . .
Yes, the kids in room _____
Are out of sight!

## Class Constitution

**MATERIALS**

"Our Class Is the Place to Be" song

chart paper or poster board

The Constitution of the United States was ratified on September 17, 1787. Create your own classroom constitution at the beginning of the school year to celebrate the anniversary of this historical event and establish agreed-upon classroom guidelines. Brainstorm with students characteristics of a cooperative classroom, sing the song below, and then use guided discussion to establish classroom rules for making that classroom a reality. Record on chart paper or poster board the following sentence frame: *We, the students of room ___, in order to have a wonderful year, write this constitution.* Record the rules that the class established, and invite all students to sign the finished document. Post it in the room for all to view and revisit.

**Class Constitution**

We, the students of room 16, in order to have a wonderful year, write this constitution:

1. Keep our hands to ourselves.
2. Use "indoor" voices.
3. Be kind to others.
4. Be good listeners.
5. Do our best!

Todd  Mick  Tana
Cooper  Jeff  Kerry
Chris  Micaela
Heidi  Sam
Julie  Oakley

 **Our Class Is the Place to Be**
*(sing to the tune of "Personality")*

Our class is the place to be.
We have a mighty fine time.
Sharing with others
Makes us feel so fine.

Kindness and laughter,
A helping hand to lend . . .
Yes, our class is the place to be
'Cause we're the living end!

And we've got . . .
Personality!

Walk with personality.
Talk with personality.
Charm and personality.
Brains and personality.
Love and personality.
And of course we've got a great big
Smi-i-ile.

So join in our good times.
The best in life is free.
Just smile and be happy.
That's the way life ought to be.

## School Is Cool! Mural

Copy the "There's Magic" chant below on a large sheet of butcher paper for a class mural, and teach it to the class. Ask students what they like most about school or what they look forward to most this year at school. Record student responses on sentence strips. Invite each student to paint on a sheet of butcher paper a picture of what he or she likes about school or looks forward to doing, seeing, or learning. When the paint dries, have students trace around their drawing with a black marker so it will stand out better. Have students cut out their drawing and glue it to the class mural. Glue the sentence strips near the related drawings. Title the mural *We Love School because School Is Cool!*

**There's Magic**
*(chant to a calypso beat)*

There's magic, there's magic
When we go to school
'Cause we're always learning
And learning is cool.

There's no end in sight
To the magic within.
If we try our best,
We know we'll always win.

ABCs and numbers
Are just the start.
Sharing with others,
We always do our part.

Learning makes us happy
And eager for more.
There's magic in learning.
It makes us want to soar.

There's magic, there's magic
When we go to school
'Cause we're always learning
And learning is cool.

There's no end in sight
To the magic within.
If we try our best,
We know we'll always win.
We know we'll always win.

## Love Dust

### MATERIALS

"Shake a Little
Love Dust" song

clear sugar or salt shaker

heart stickers

rice (dyed pink and red) or
heart-shaped confetti

glue

Decorate a sugar or salt shaker with heart stickers, and fill the shaker with pink and red rice or heart-shaped confetti. (Be sure the rice is bigger than the holes on the shaker.) Glue the lid closed. Explain to students that you have "love dust" and the love dust spreads love in the room. Sing the song "Shake a Little Love Dust" as you sprinkle love dust on your students. Use the love dust when someone has used an unloving word, when someone is sad, or when your class needs a little boost of love. It will encourage students to reach out in love.

**Shake a Little Love Dust**
*(sing to the tune of "The Muffin Man")*

Shake a little love dust, love dust, love dust.
Shake a little love dust, and brighten up your day.

Love dust makes us happy, happy, happy.
Love dust makes us happy in each and every way.

Share a little love dust, love dust, love dust.
Share a little love dust, and this is what you'll say . . .

(Repeat from the beginning)

## Love at Home

### MATERIALS

"Love Can" poem

heart-shaped tin or small tin decorated with heart stickers

Love Dust
(see page 14)

blank heart-shaped journal

Write *Love Can* and the "Love Can" poem on a heart-shaped tin or small tin decorated with heart stickers. You can also place "love dust" inside the tin. Write on one side of the tin *Ingredients: kind words, thoughtful deeds, good manners, gentle ways, patience, honesty, "sharefulness," and smiles.* Discuss ways the students can share love with others both at school and at home. Invite each class member to take turns taking home the "love can" and a heart-shaped journal. Have the student discuss with his or her family how they share love or how sharing love made a difference and record it in the "Love Journal." Students and their families will enjoy reading all the different ways they share love.

### Love Can

This can of love will season
All your days with laughs and cheer
If you use it generously
On your friends throughout the year!

## Smile!

### MATERIALS

"Upside-Down Frown" song

construction paper

crayons or markers

glue

wiggly eyes

scissors

brass fasteners

Discuss with students how smiles can help them feel happy. Encourage students to share a smile with a friend. Teach them the song "Upside-Down Frown." Copy the song onto a sheet of construction paper for each student. Have students draw a head on it and glue on two wiggly eyes. Invite students to cut out a big U shape for a smile from another sheet of construction paper. Help students use a brass fastener to add a smile to their face. Students will love turning the frown upside down into a smile!

### Upside-Down Frown
*(sing to the tune of a jazzy "Jingle Bells")*

Take a frown
Turn it upside down.
And smile your worries away.
Sad times turn to glad times
If you practice smiling all day.

# MIGHTY MANNERS

Reciting songs and poems about good manners teaches students to act appropriately as situations arise in the classroom and on the playground. Use the following poems and songs as tools for behavior management. Using poetry and song to handle crisis situations tends to defuse emotion and bring students back to task in a loving manner.

## What a Mess!

**MATERIALS**
"It's Time to Clean Up!" song

Teach the song "It's Time to Clean Up!" to your students. This is a great song to sing as students clean up the classroom.

 **It's Time to Clean Up!**
*(sing to the tune of "Shortening Bread")*

It's time to clean up, clean up, clean up,
It's time to clean up. Please, clean up now.

Put away the _____, _____, _____,
Put away the _____. Clean up now.

Everybody's helping, yes sir-ee.
Everybody's helping, it's plain to see.

## One for Me and One for You

Discuss how nice it feels to have someone share. Teach the song "Sharing" to your students. Have students cut out the song and glue it to construction paper. Invite each student to color and cut out a strip from the Sharing Toys reproducible. Have each student draw on the construction paper a self-portrait and a picture of a friend on opposite sides of the paper and carefully cut a 2" (5 cm) vertical slit next to each picture as shown. Show students how to slide their strip into the slits so the toy bear is shared between the two friends.

## Mirror, Mirror, on the Wall

In advance, cut out a Mirror pattern for each student and cut an aluminum-foil circle to fit in the center of each one. Discuss with students the importance of treating others the way they want to be treated. Explain to students that sometimes we can see how well we are treating others by the way others are responding to us. Other people can act as a reflection of us. For example, if we are generous to others, other people will often be generous to us. If we smile often, others will often smile back. Invite students to glue an aluminum-foil circle to their pattern to make a "mirror." This can remind them of how they need to look at themselves and how they treat others. Teach students the song "Watch What You Say!" Have students glue their mirror and the song to a sheet of construction paper.

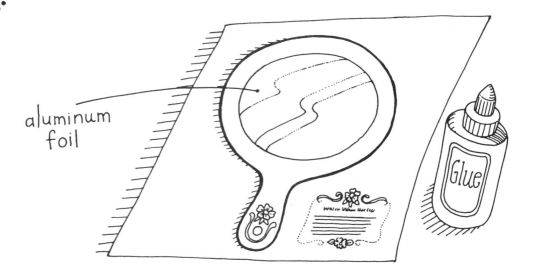

aluminum foil

# Kind Words Here

Discuss with students how telling secrets can hurt others' feelings by leaving them out. Teach your students the song "Secrets." Brainstorm with students kind words and phrases that include others. Write the words and phrases on heart cutouts, and place them in a pocket chart for reference and word recognition. Provide each student with an envelope labeled *Kind Words* and a copy of the Kind Words reproducible. Have students cut out the words and place them in their envelope. Tell students to use their kind words toward others as often as they can.

### Secrets
*(sing to the tune of "Up on the Rooftop")*

Tell a secret?
No, not me.
I include everyone.
Don't you see?
Leaving others out
Makes them sad.
I only share kindness,
Making others glad.

*Chorus:*
Tell a secret?
No, not me.
Tell a secret?
No, sir-ee.
I think of others in everything I do.
I think of others,
And I hope that you will, too.

## Garbage Talk

Give each student a copy of the Garbage Can reproducible. Teach students the song "Into the Garbage." Invite students to color the garbage can and cut it out. Have students glue their garbage can cutout to a sheet of construction paper. Read the words in the sun shapes with students, and discuss how using these "sunshine" words makes people feel good. Have students glue tissue-paper pieces to the top of their garbage can to represent "ugly" words. Remind students to throw away their ugly words and use sunshine words instead.

Terrific!
Fine!
Wow!
Please!
Hello!

**Into the Garbage**
(sing to the tune of "You Are My Sunshine")

Words that are hurtful
Go in the trash can.
We want to clean them
Out of our way.
We'll only use our
Sunshine words to
Brighten every day.

Into the garbage
Go ugly words that
Make our friends feel
So very sad.
Instead we'll use our
Sunshine words to
Make all of us feel glad.

Super!
Sweet!
Awesome!
Cool!
Great!

## Our Handiwork

Teach the song "My Hands" to your class. Have each student trace one hand on a piece of construction paper and cut it out. Ask students what good things they can do with their hands, and record their responses on sentence strips. Invite students to draw on their hand cutout a picture of something they can do with their hands. Display the song on a bulletin board, and post the cutouts and the sentence strips around it.

**My Hands**
(sing to the tune of "Oats, Peas, Beans, and Barley Grow")

Sometimes my hands are naughty,
And so my mother says
That she will have to scold them
And send them off to bed.
So, little hands, be careful in everything you do,
'Cause if you have to go to bed,
I do, too!!

Shake hands.

Hug.

Comb my hair.

Pet my dog.

Pick up trash.

## Sing like a Bird

### MATERIALS

"Whenever You're Angry" song (page 21)

construction-paper circles

glue

scissors

large white construction-paper ovals

brass fasteners

wiggly eyes

candy corn

feathers (available at craft stores)

construction paper

crayons or markers

Teach the song "Whenever You're Angry" to your students. Discuss how anger can some-times result in saying and doing things that we do not mean. Explain how singing can help lessen that anger. Invite each student to glue two construction-paper circles on top of each other to make a bird body. Ask each student to cut a large white construction-paper oval in half horizontally to make a hatching "egg." Have students slightly overlap their oval halves and insert a brass fastener to the left side as a hinge so the egg opens and closes. Tell students to glue their bird body behind the egg bottom so the bird is revealed when the top part of the egg is moved up. Have each student glue on wiggly eyes, a candy-corn beak, and feathers. Invite students to glue a copy of the song "Whenever You're Angry" on the outside of their egg. Have students glue their egg to construction paper. Invite students to draw music notes around their bird.

## Oops!

### MATERIALS

"Accidents Can Happen" song (page 26)

Tell students about a time when you had an accident. Explain how acci-dents can happen to anyone. Teach your students the song "Accidents Can Happen." Give students a copy of the song, and have them try to find as many accidents as they can in the picture.

## My Manners Chart

### MATERIALS

My Manners Chart reproducible (page 27)

stickers (optional)

Give each student a copy of the My Manners Chart reproducible. Discuss the different ways students can use good manners. Review each statement on the reproducible. Invite students to take the chart home, talk over their school day with their family, and record their use of good manners with a sticker or smiley face each day.

# Sharing

*(sing to the tune of "Six Little Ducks")*

I always like to share my toys

With the other little girls and boys.

Because sharing is the nicest way

To have a good time when I play.

# Whenever You're Angry

*(sing to the tune of "Rock-a-Bye Baby")*

Whenever you're angry,

Be like a bird.

Sing just a little,

But don't say a word.

# Sharing Toys

# Mirror

## Watch What You Say!

*(sing to the tune of "Pop! Goes the Weasel")*

Sassy Frassy, watch what you say.
You need to be kind in every way.
Show respect and courtesy, too,
Because how you treat others
Is how they'll treat you.

# Kind Words

You're sweet.

You worked hard.

Good job.

I like you.

You're my friend.

Good try!

Thank you.

You are nice.

Do you want to play?

Let's be friends.

I'm glad to know you.

You make me smile.

# Garbage Can

Terrific!

Fine!

Wow!

Please!

Hello!

## Into the Garbage

*(sing to the tune of "You Are My Sunshine")*

Words that are hurtful
Go in the trash can.
We want to clean them
Out of our way.
We'll only use our
Sunshine words to
Brighten every day.

Into the garbage
Go ugly words that
Make our friends feel
So very sad.
Instead we'll use our
Sunshine words to
Make all of us feel glad.

Super!

Sweet!

Awesome!

Cool!

Great!

# Accidents Can Happen

*(sing to the tune of "Supercalifragilisticexpialidocious")*

Accidents can happen,

They happen every day.

Accidents can happen,

And when they do I say,

"I'm sorry. I'm sorry.

I didn't mean to do it.

I'm sorry. I'm sorry.

I guess I really blew it!"

*The Creative K–1 Classroom © 1999 Creative Teaching Press*

## My Manners Chart

| | Mon. | Tues. | Wed. | Thurs. | Fri. | Mon. | Tues. | Wed. | Thurs. | Fri. |
|---|---|---|---|---|---|---|---|---|---|---|
| I talked with a quiet voice. | | | | | | | | | | |
| I did not interrupt. | | | | | | | | | | |
| I said "Please" and "Thank you." | | | | | | | | | | |
| I did not run in the house. | | | | | | | | | | |
| I did my chores. | | | | | | | | | | |
| I did not argue or fight. | | | | | | | | | | |
| I was kind to my family. | | | | | | | | | | |
| I obeyed my parents. | | | | | | | | | | |
| I said "I'm sorry" when it was appropriate. | | | | | | | | | | |
| I waited my turn. | | | | | | | | | | |
| I listened to my teacher. | | | | | | | | | | |
| I followed the rules at school. | | | | | | | | | | |
| I got my work done. | | | | | | | | | | |
| I brushed my teeth. | | | | | | | | | | |
| I went to bed without complaining. | | | | | | | | | | |

# PARENT INVOLVEMENT

Get (and keep!) your parents involved by maintaining open communication and offering a variety of opportunities for them to help—inside and outside the classroom. Keep parents informed of the happenings within your classroom and the topics the class studies, and encourage parents to share their knowledge and interests with the class. Provide opportunities for parents to actively participate at their child's school. A little advance planning can make a world of difference when it comes to utilizing the skills and resources that come from your students' families.

## Class Information Booklet

Anticipate questions parents might ask, and provide them with a Classroom Information Booklet at the beginning of the school year. This will help maximize the effectiveness of your program and minimize questions and confusion. Be sure to address the following policies and procedures:

♥ Class Schedule (when school begins and ends)

♥ School Calendar (school holidays and half-days)

♥ Tardy Policy

♥ Discipline Policy

♥ Sharing Schedule

♥ Snack Policy (including appropriate foods to bring or avoid)

♥ Homework Policy (due dates, expectations of parent involvement, length of time students are expected to spend on homework, and guidelines for reading at home)

♥ Birthdays (when they are celebrated, types of treats to bring, "un-birthdays," and policy for birthday invitations)

♥ Celebrations (other parties that are planned throughout the year)

♥ P.T.A. Events

♥ Penmanship Guidelines

♥ Pick-up or Drop-off Information

♥ Newsletters (when they are sent out)

## Class Directory

Distribute a class list of addresses and phone numbers to parents so they can send birthday invitations, contact volunteers, or invite students over to play. Be sure to obtain parent permission before including addresses and phone numbers in a class list. Have parents complete the Directory form (page 34), and then compile the information in a class directory.

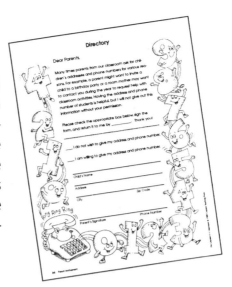

## Walking Field Trips

Many enriching and educational opportunities are available right outside your door. You can plan some walks in advance, but there may be times when you would like to take a more spontaneous walk. Send home a form at the beginning of the year for parents to sign, giving their child permission to join the class on walking trips in the neighborhood. Have parents include an emergency phone number, too. Invite family members to join the class on walking trips and keep you informed of anything special the class could explore in the neighborhood.

## Guest Speakers

After completing your School Calendar (see page 5), recruit parents and community members to participate in your program. Reproduce the Guest Speakers form (page 35) or create your own "wish list" of services that would benefit your program, and distribute it on Back-to-School Night or Welcome Day. When parents choose an area that they are interested in, sign them up on your School Calendar. Since you already recorded on the calendar when you will cover different themes, you can immediately plan a date for the volunteers to visit the classroom. This long-range planning will greatly increase the number of enriching participants in your program.

## Welcome Day

Before school begins, invite your students and their parents to a Welcome Day. This allows students to get acquainted with the classroom and your routines before school begins so on the first day you can all get off to a great start. It also gives parents the opportunity to meet you and complete important forms. Prepare a few activities for students to do while parents complete forms. For example, have students create the first bulletin board (or front door decoration) by having each student place one hand on a paint-soaked sponge and then place it on butcher paper. The students can sign their name next to their hand-print. Title the display *The Students in Room ____ Are Handled with Care*. This gives students ownership of the room when they arrive the first day of school.

To make sure that all families see and do everything you would like them to, create a self-guided tour that spotlights your classroom program. Draw a map that corresponds to the areas in your classroom you want families to see. See the Self-Guided Tour on page 36 as an example. This is the perfect opportunity to have parents complete the Guest Speakers form (page 35) and the Directory form (page 34). Ask an aide, a parent volunteer, or a past student to be at the front door, greet parents, give them a copy of the self-guided tour, and answer questions. This frees you to interact freely with parents and students.

## Prescriptive Teaching

When parents drop in to help, invite them to use your Prescriptive Teaching basket (see page 58) to work with students. Write on index cards student names and the skill they need to practice. For example, five students may need to learn how to tie their shoes, so their names would be on an index card labeled *Tie shoes*. Other students may not know the /b/ sound, so their names would be on an index card labeled *Letter sound /b/*. Have volunteers review the index cards, choose a skill to work on, and use the assessment materials in the basket (e.g., a baby shoe to tie or letter and picture cards for letter sound practice) to work on that skill with students either individually or in small groups. Include directions for the volunteers on how to do the practice activity. Ask volunteers to place a checkmark after the student name once the student has mastered the skill. Periodically update the cards and reassess student skills.

## Student-Led Conferences

Prior to conferences, send home the Conference Letter (page 37) to let parents know what to expect during the conference. In advance, prepare a program for parents. Use the Student-Led Conference Program (page 38) and the Center Activities (page 39) as examples. Prepare activities at each center for students to complete with their parents. Adapt the activity ideas to fit your program. Conduct your conferences in the same way as learning centers (see Creating and Managing Centers on page 149), signing up three families at the same time with one-hour intervals between each group.

Have students accompany their parents. Upon arriving, ask families to pick up a program and move from center to center with the student demonstrating his or her level of competence on specific grade-level skills. Families may start at whichever center they want. Pull one family aside at a time to conference with you. Do not feel that you have to wait for them to finish the program before meeting with you; do it at your convenience. There is no need to feel rushed. Keep it casual, comfortable, and homey. You will actually have time to visit and interact with each family during the hour. By the time the parents meet with you, they have already seen samples of student work and become aware of what their child can and cannot do. This makes your job much easier and actually decreases the amount of time required for each conference.

During each conference, encourage parents to list items that they will commit to work on at home with their child. When parents are finished meeting with you, they are free to leave. Conferencing in this manner allows the students to be part of the process. Once you feel comfortable with the procedure, you will find that you can actually schedule four families each hour and still have time to become well acquainted with each one.

## Calling All Volunteers

Encourage parents to volunteer in the classroom and take an active role in their child's learning. You will find that parent volunteers will be easier to arrange for if you schedule classroom needs around the parents' schedules. For example, the first hour or the last hour of the day is generally much easier for a parent than an hour in the middle of the day. Also, be willing to have younger siblings in the classroom. Babysitting is often an important reason why a parent will not be able to help. Schedule your day so parents can sign up for the same time each day or each week. Parents make great resources at classroom centers. They can help give extra attention to small groups while you work with one group or individual students. Ask parents to commit to a time to come in on a weekly, biweekly, or daily basis on the Volunteer Sign-Up sheet (page 40). Display the Parent Volunteers sheet (page 41) in class so volunteers can use it to help find substitutes when they are unable to come in. Ask parents to also complete the Volunteer Record (page 40) prior to working in your classroom. This will help you keep a record of important information about your volunteers.

## Project Box

Many parents who are unable to work in the classroom are happy to help out from home. The trick is to be sufficiently organized so you can have materials ready to go home several weeks before they are needed. Place a "to-do box" (or basket) by the door so parents do not need to interrupt you when they come to class. Label each item with instructions, provide a completed sample, and place a copy of a Project Ticket (page 42) with the item. Include the date by which you need the project returned. The parent signs the Project Ticket and leaves it in the box or basket so you can track the item if needed. When the work is returned, throw out the ticket.

## Parent Training

Set aside a time to train your parent volunteers. Write out a sheet with guide-lines for the volunteers. Use the Training Checklist (page 43) as a guide. Give a copy to your volunteers for them to take notes on. Explain where volunteers go when they arrive, what they do, and where to place their personal belong-ings. Provide a sign-in/sign-out sheet. You may also consider giving them name tags to wear. Discuss the activities that students will do at each learn-ing center. Emphasize that the class counts on them to keep their commit-ment. If they cannot make it, they need to find a substitute. Remind parents to dress appropriately, work quietly, and not do students' work. Teach parents to ask questions in response to students' questions. For example, parents might ask *What did your teacher say? What do you think? What are your friends doing? What would a Whiz Kid do?* Ask parents to look over students' penmanship and check that all students are holding their pencils correctly. Remind parents that they are the teachers at their center and deserve respect. Tell volunteers not to add *okay?* to the end of a statement, as that can lead to students refusing to do a job. Also, stress the importance of volunteers respecting confidentiality. Finally, remind volunteers that students must clean up when finished.

## Open House

Make certain your visitors see a sampling of everything the students have worked on throughout the year. Display special reports or projects, a science project, and an activity such as Edit and Eat (see page 169) for visitors to par-ticipate in. Draw attention to bulletin boards, artwork, class books, individual anthologies of writing, and memory books. Provide parents with a program similar to the one for Welcome Day (see page 30) that directs them through a self-guided tour. Provide activities, like Center Activities (see page 39), at each center. Have a class video playing in the background.

# Directory

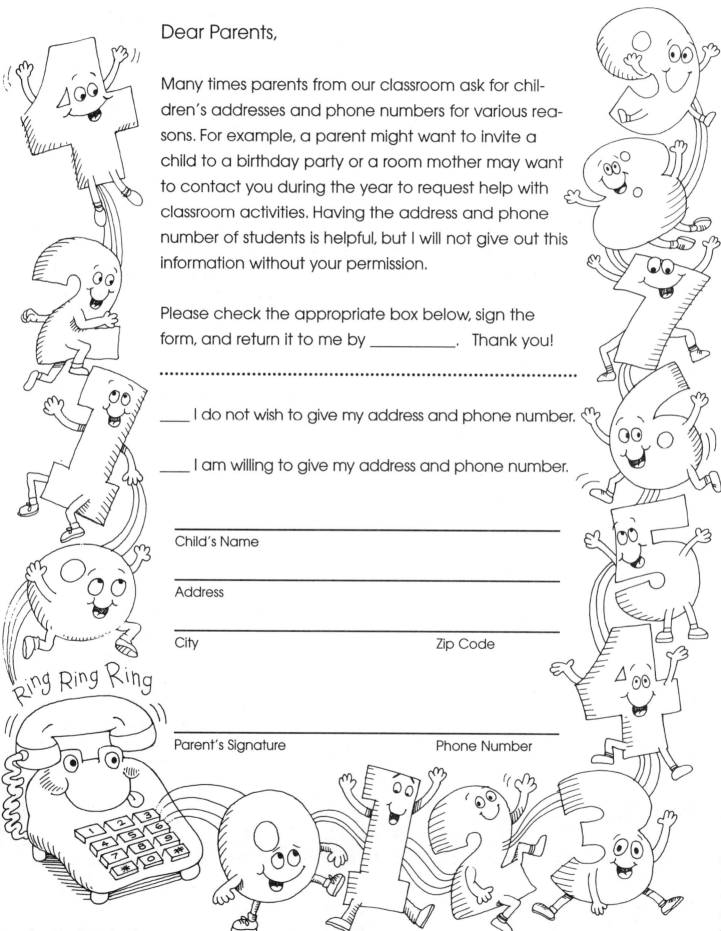

Dear Parents,

Many times parents from our classroom ask for children's addresses and phone numbers for various reasons. For example, a parent might want to invite a child to a birthday party or a room mother may want to contact you during the year to request help with classroom activities. Having the address and phone number of students is helpful, but I will not give out this information without your permission.

Please check the appropriate box below, sign the form, and return it to me by _____.   Thank you!

....................................................................

____ I do not wish to give my address and phone number.

____ I am willing to give my address and phone number.

_____
Child's Name

_____
Address

_____
City                                                    Zip Code

_____
Parent's Signature                          Phone Number

Ring Ring Ring

# Guest Speakers

Dear Parents,

I am eager to make this year the best educational experience possible for your child. For this reason, I am looking for people with special skills and interests to enrich our program. Family and friends serve as excellent resources. I hope you will share your interests and knowledge with us and spread the word to your friends and relatives. All contributions are greatly appreciated.

Please circle each item that you have a special interest in or knowledge about and would be willing to share with us. Return this list to me as soon as possible so we can start making arrangements. Thank you for your support. It's going to be a wonderful year!

| | | | |
|---|---|---|---|
| Acrobat | Dentist | Hula Dancer | Pilot |
| African American | Doctor | Juggler | Pirate |
| Antique Collector | Engineer | Abraham Lincoln | Police Officer |
| Artist | Eskimo | Magician | Polynesian |
| Astronaut | Farmer | Miner | Post Office Worker |
| Astronomer | Firefighter | Musician | Reptile Handler |
| Author | Ben Franklin | Native American | Santa Claus |
| Blacksmith | Gardener | Naturalist | Sign Language |
| Carpenter | Giant | Oceanographer | Veterinarian |
| Chinese American | Hearing-Impaired | Paper Maker | Visually Impaired |
| Clown | Person | Physically Challenged | Person |
| Cowboy | Hero | Person | George Washington |
| Dancer | Horse and Trainer | Pilgrim | Zookeeper |

Other: _____

Do you have access to any special collections? If so, what are they? _____

Thank you for all your support!

# Self-Guided Tour

## Welcome to our class!

Please use this page as a guided tour of the classroom. Our intent is to introduce your child to important aspects of our program. You will find a few things to do along the way, so please take a pencil with you to keep track of each item completed.

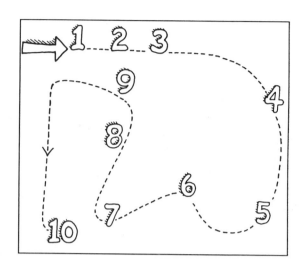

1. **Coatracks**—All jackets and sweaters are kept on the racks during class.

2. **Snack Box**—Snacks should be left here each morning as each child enters the room. Please send a snack on the first day of school.

3. **Cubby**—You will find a headband with your child's name on it in his or her cubby. Please measure it on your child's head, staple it together, and replace it in the cubby.

4. **Think and Do Center**—While your child plays with a few activities here, please take a few minutes to fill out the Directory form.

5. **Math Center**—Invite your child to play at this table while you sign up for a convenient assessment time.

6. **Sharing Shelf**—Items brought to school for sharing will be placed on this shelf.

7. **Literacy Center**—Please browse through the Guest Speakers form. If there is anything that you are able to share with our class, it would be greatly welcomed. Also, if you know others who would be interested in sharing their talents or knowledge with the class, we can promise them an exciting experience.

8. **ABC Center**—While your child is busy doing the activity, please fill out the Volunteer Sign-Up sheet. Make certain your child writes his or her name on the activity paper.

9. **Teacher's Basket**—This is where your child places all completed work and notes from home. Please show your child the basket and place the Directory form, Guest Speakers form, Volunteer Sign-Up sheet, and student work in the basket.

10. **Me**—Please don't forget to say hello to me before you leave the room.

11. **Restrooms**—Please walk your child to the restrooms.

12. **Pencils**—Kindly return the pencil used to check off this list.

13. **Playground**—Feel free to walk your child to the playground area. Refreshments will be served.

Thank you for coming. It's going to be a great year!

*The Creative K–1 Classroom* © 1999 Creative Teaching Press

# Conference Letter

Dear Parents,

It is time for conferences. The students and I are eager to share with you how much they have learned during the year. Our time together will be exciting and informative, I assure you.

Please note the following:
- Though three or four families will be signed up for the same time slot, you will still receive a private conference with me.
- Your child should accompany you to the conference.
- Please try to make other arrangements for siblings, since this is your child's special time and other families will be in the room as well.
- Please arrive on time and plan to stay for one hour.

I'm looking forward to spending this time with you and your child.

Your child's teacher,

_____

# Student-Led Conference Program

Dear Parents,

This student-led conference is designed to provide you with the opportunity to see firsthand how and what your child is learning in class. During the next hour, you will participate in the type of learning activities that are part of your child's daily routine. Please plan to spend at least ten minutes at each center, ten minutes looking at your child's work, and ten minutes of conference time with me. Monitor and adjust your time as needed.

Please note the following:
- Centers do not need to be visited in sequence.
- Select one or more of the activities listed in each center.
- Record below any questions or comments about your child's work as you proceed.
- Note below what your child needs to work on.
- Generously praise and encourage your child.

Enjoy this time together. I'm looking forward to visiting with you.

Questions/Comments

_____

_____

_____

_____

Things to Work On

_____

_____

_____

The Creative K–1 Classroom © 1999 Creative Teaching Press

# Center Activities

## 123 Math Center

1. Have your child use the colored counters, blocks, or linking cubes and graph paper to make a graph.

2. Have your child glue the cutout shapes to the paper to make a pattern.

3. Have your child place the magnetic numbers in order.

4. Have your child count the coins and read their values.

## ABC ABC Center

1. Have your child match objects that rhyme.

2. Ask your child to sort the objects in the tubs according to beginning sounds.

3. Have your child match alphabet noodles to their corresponding lowercase letters on the reproducible.

4. Ask your child to read to you from the rhyme-family flowers.

## Child's Work

1. Please take your child's folder and accompanying materials.

2. Find a comfortable place to review these materials with your child.

3. Be generous with praise and encouragement.

##  Literacy Center

1. Ask your child to read the sentences in the pocket chart.

2. Ask your child to read a mini-book from his or her storybook box.

3. Have your child sequence the story cards and retell the story.

## Think and Do Center

1. Ask your child to tie the shoe.

2. Have your child use scissors to cut out the pattern.

3. Ask your child to sort the objects in the tub and explain the categories to you.

4. Go outside with your child and ask him or her to jump rope, climb the ladder, use the slide, walk the balance beam, or practice ball-handling skills.

# Volunteer Sign-Up

Name _____

Address _____

_____

Phone Number _____

I am available on _____ from _____ to _____
　　　　　　　　　　　day(s) of week　　　　　　　　　　time　　　　　　　time
to help out in the classroom.

I prefer to:

____ Do prep work around the classroom.　　　　____ Work with small groups.

____ Do prep work at home each week.　　　　　____ Help with special events and celebrations.

____ Work with individual students.　　　　　　____ Other: _____

- - - - - - - - - - - - - - - - - - - - - - - - - - - - - - - - - - - - - - - - - - - -

# Volunteer Record

Name _____

Address _____

_____

Phone Number _____

Special Skills _____

_____

Hobbies _____

Person to contact in an emergency:

Name _____

Phone Number _____

# Parent Volunteers

| | Name | Time | Phone Number |
|---|---|---|---|
| Monday | | | |
| | | | |
| | | | |
| Tuesday | | | |
| | | | |
| | | | |
| Wednesday | | | |
| | | | |
| | | | |
| Thursday | | | |
| | | | |
| | | | |
| Friday | | | |
| | | | |
| | | | |

Room Parent:

Assistants:

Available to substitute (name/phone number):

# Project Tickets

## Project Ticket

Name

Project

Date needed

Thanks for helping!

## Project Ticket

Name

Project

Date needed

Thanks for helping!

## Project Ticket

Name

Project

Date needed

Thanks for helping!

## Project Ticket

Name

Project

Date needed

Thanks for helping!

# Training Checklist

Please feel free to take notes on this paper.

**Our Routine**

Sign in.

Wear a name tag.

"Where do I go?" "What do I do?"

Personal Belongings

**Regular Activities**

Math Center

Literacy Center

ABC Center

Think and Do Center

**Guidelines**

Dress appropriately.

Students stay in center for duration.

Have students work quietly.

Do NOT do students' work.

**Ask Questions in Response to Questions**

What did your teacher say?

What do you think?

What are your friends doing?

What would a Whiz Kid do?

**Penmanship**

Be sure students are holding their pencils correctly.

**Remember**

We count on you! If you can't come, please find a substitute.

Be confidential!

You are the teacher, and you deserve respect.

How to respond to "I don't want to!" (Say "I'm sorry. This is your work, but when you're done you may . . . .")

Don't include "okay?" at the end of your sentences.

Make sure students clean up after each activity.

# GETTING A GRIP ON BEHAVIOR

Minimize behavior problems by developing a class spirit of respect and cooperation. Implement strategies and techniques that increase student interest, participation, and responsibility by focusing energy in a positive manner. There is no one method of dealing with behavior problems. No single strategy of intervention works every time. However, there are several strategies that work effectively in different situations. Try some of the following strategies to help redirect negative behavior.

## Set Your Expectations

It seems like a silly question, but do you know what it is you expect from your students? Do you expect them to sit quietly while you are speaking? Do you expect them to take care of classroom materials and to pick up after themselves? Do you expect them to be kind to their friends? Before we can expect well-mannered students, we need to know what it is we expect from them. Once we have determined what that is, we need to convey that message effectively to the students and teach them to be accountable for that behavior.

For the most part, students are willing to be cooperative and well behaved. But when a student does not comply with a teacher's expectations, it is often due to one of three things:

♥ The student does not know what behavior is expected.

♥ The student lacks respect for the teacher and the teacher's ability to lead effectively.

♥ A task is too easy or too hard, resulting in boredom or frustration.

When a teacher effectively addresses each of these issues, behavior management becomes incidental to the other activities in the classroom. A positive tone can be maintained because the focus is on learning, not on controlling behavior.

## What Effective Teachers Do

An effective teacher treats each student with dignity, uses a soft voice and gentle ways, teaches students to be responsible for their own behavior, and never resorts to ridicule or embarrassment. An effective teacher knows that busy, interested students are seldom behavior problems. An effective teacher respects the learning styles of each student and provides a variety of high-interest activities to keep students focused on worthwhile goals.

## Set the Standard

Determine your expectations for your class. Be consistent, firm, and fair. Be sure to match your activities and requirements with your students' capabilities. Behavior problems are often a result of the teacher's failure to adapt his or her instruction to the students' abilities. The following tips ought to ensure you get quality work from your students instead of "scribble, scribble, done."

## 12 Steps to Empowering Yourself

Apply the following tips to empower yourself and maintain control of your classroom:

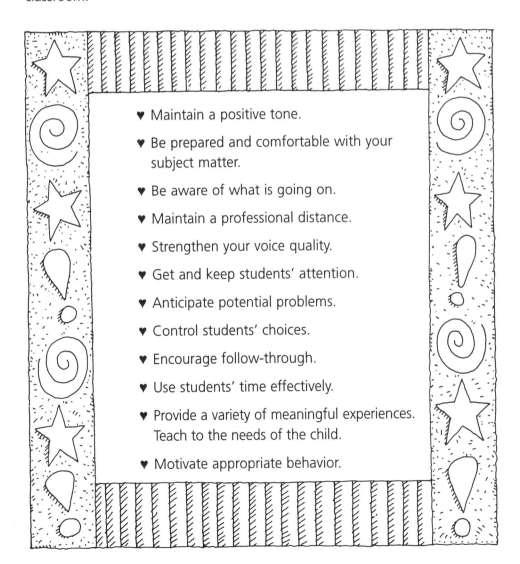

- ♥ Maintain a positive tone.
- ♥ Be prepared and comfortable with your subject matter.
- ♥ Be aware of what is going on.
- ♥ Maintain a professional distance.
- ♥ Strengthen your voice quality.
- ♥ Get and keep students' attention.
- ♥ Anticipate potential problems.
- ♥ Control students' choices.
- ♥ Encourage follow-through.
- ♥ Use students' time effectively.
- ♥ Provide a variety of meaningful experiences. Teach to the needs of the child.
- ♥ Motivate appropriate behavior.

## Problem Solving

Use conflict resolution skills with your students. Explain and reinforce the following strategies when conflicts arise:

- Talk it over.
- If something seems wrong, and you can't fix it, just walk away.
- Let everyone play.
- Take turns.
- Use kind words.
- Share.
- Be quick to forgive.
- Ask for help.

## Cool-off Time

Provide a place for students to go when they are on the verge of losing self-control, such as a "thinking chair" in a quiet area of the room. Give them a couple of minutes to think about how they can act differently, and when they are ready to rejoin the group, they may. Having a place for them to cool off is an important strategy. If you remove students who want attention from their audience, you take away their reward. If you are consistent, they will learn to modify their behavior. It also keeps you from becoming angry and losing your own self-control.

## Attention Grabbers

Each teacher needs to find the best way to get and keep the class's attention. Some turn lights on and off, ring bells, or open a music box to get the class's attention. Singing is one favored way to get students to join in. Whatever needs to be said can just as easily be sung. The melodic sound of a voice is an instant attention grabber. Sing the song "Clean Up" (below) with your students during transitions. When kids are squirrelly, invite them to sing "Head, Shoulders, Knees, and Toes" or another song with large body movements.

### Clean Up
*(sing to the tune of "Paw-Paw Patch")*

Clean up, pick up, put away.
Leave no sign you were here today.
Act like a pixie and be of good cheer
So no one will know that you were ever here.

## Brownie Points

When students are behaving well, hold up your pointer finger, touch it to your tongue, and make a tally mark in the air. Tell students they just received a brownie point for their good behavior. Continue making tally marks in the air as students demonstrate good behavior. Students enjoy the recognition for their good behavior. There is no need to keep an accurate number of points, but when the students ask how many brownie points they have, demonstrate with outstretched arms. When they have earned "enough," celebrate with popcorn or a picnic lunch. (If for any reason students have acted inappropriately, pantomime erasing a point and feeling sad.)

## Nonverbal Techniques

At the beginning stages of misbehavior, nonverbal techniques can be an effective way of letting students know that they need to settle down. Use eye contact, body posture, proximity, facial expressions, and silence to regain attention. Never talk when someone else is talking. Stop teaching. Use a "magic sign," such as holding up two fingers while waiting for the class to quiet down and hold up their fingers. Verbal techniques can also be effective, but are so overused that their long-term impact seems questionable. Use a "poker face" when redirecting students' behavior so they know you mean what you say.

## Physical Proximity

Get close to disruptive students. Merely walking up to and standing beside a disruptive student can frequently bring about a desired result. A gentle touch on a shoulder without a word will often quiet a disruptive student. Most students will get the message.

## Take It Away

Remove the source of a disturbance. Silently take away rubber bands, toys, food, or other items that cause distractions. Sometimes there are phenomena that students are naturally interested in and will give their attention to, such as hailstorms, sirens, a new student teacher, or a student's new shoes or haircut. When these attractions capture students' attention, allow a few minutes of exploration. It is impossible to compete with some events.

## Assign a Task

Give a disruptive student a job to do. For example, ask him or her for help carrying books from one place to another. Carrying heavy objects helps calm students down, and helping you helps redirect their behavior.

## Change the Activity

When the class is acting up, it is probably time to change the activity. Prevent behavior problems by ensuring that your activities are meaningful and relevant. Dreary classrooms, monotonous routines, irrelevant content, and tedious work will increase the incidence of bad attitude and inappropriate behavior.

## Sing a Song

Break out in song. As students chime in, you will again have their attention. Teach songs to your class early in the year so the class can join you in singing a repertoire of songs. Sing songs that apply as situations arise. For example, when someone spills on another student's art project, sing the song "Accidents Can Happen" (see page 26).

## Change Your Voice

You can often obtain students' attention by altering the tone, pitch, volume, or speed of your voice. Voice suspension, which means you slow down your speech and pause between each word, can be effective. For example, say *It . . . is . . . almost . . . time . . . for . . . recess.* You may also speak in a whisper so students need to quiet down to hear you. Speak in a sing-song voice to get their attention. Without talking down to students, you may try using a more dramatic voice. Be sure not to belittle students by drawing attention to their mistakes. Subtlety is key to gaining students' respect, which is probably the most important preventative strategy of all.

## Laugh

Whoever said, "Don't smile until Christmas"? Forget it. Smile, smile, and smile some more. Laughter is healthy in the classroom. Allow yourself to find humor in situations. Be willing to laugh at yourself. Enjoy your students and laugh along with them.

## A Pat on the Back

Choose a reward for good student behavior. Be sure that your rules are clear and that the system is fair and consistently followed. Good behavior is not necessarily its own reward. The quickest and surest way of eliminating misbehavior is rewarding its opposite.

## Self-Evaluation

If certain students need extra guidance and accountability with their daily behavior, help them complete the Self-Evaluation (page 52). Having students fill it out helps them take responsibility for their behavior. Send home the form to keep parents informed about student behavior.

## Sign Language

Use a few sign-language signs for classroom control. The advantage to sign language is that you can be talking to the class with your voice and to one individual with your hands. It is particularly handy when a child needs to go to the bathroom—a single wave of the t-sign for toilet and he or she is off. No big deal.

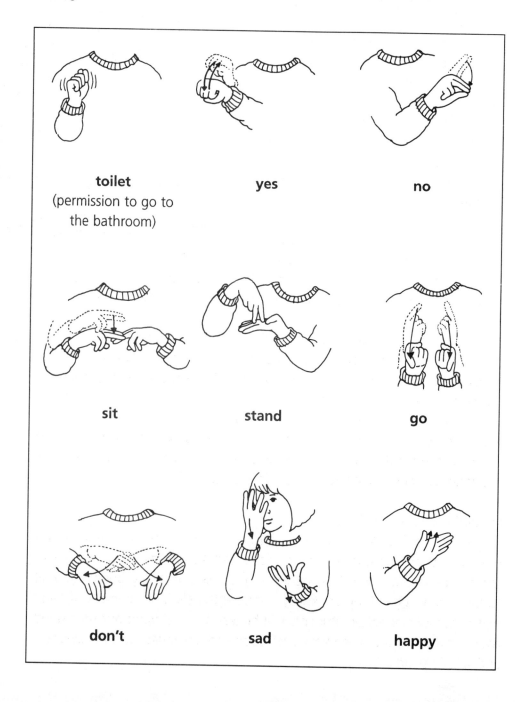

**toilet**
(permission to go to
the bathroom)

**yes**

**no**

**sit**

**stand**

**go**

**don't**

**sad**

**happy**

## Whiz Kid Work

If students are expected to do their best work, do not accept anything less. A few simple policies go a long way to making excellence a habit.

- Decide what your expectations are, and make those expectations clear to your students. For example, students have their name on their paper, they have done their best (Whiz Kid work), they work quietly and independently, and they take pride in their accomplishments.
- Stress how lucky you feel because everyone in your class is a Whiz Kid.
- Walk among the students and compliment their Whiz Kid work.
- Only Whiz Kid work goes in the teacher's basket. Nothing but Whiz Kid work is accepted. Other work is returned for refinement. A special stamp on seatwork confirms the student's best efforts.
- A time limit can help students do better quality work. State *Nobody's done until the ding-dong dings* or *Nobody's done until the teacher sings.* This allows you to monitor the quality of work in progress, requiring the students to slow down and use more care.
- Let students know that if there is still white on the paper, there may be something else they can add. Encourage more complex artwork.
- Acknowledge students' successes. For example, say *I like the way you were listening and following directions. I noticed how hard you were working. You used many colorful pictures on your paper.*
- Give students a copy of the Super Whiz Kid Award (page 53) when they are spotlighted for the week. Or, give awards to students who have earned a certain number of Whiz Kid Tickets (page 54).

## Invisible Acts of Kindness

Make copies of the Whiz Kid Tickets (page 54), and give them to students for unsung acts of kindness. Remind students that Whiz Kids never brag about the good deeds they do. They never make an issue of being good, but wait to be commended. They act kindly because it is the right thing to do and makes others feel better. Students will be less likely to point out their good deeds, but be sure to keep your eyes open and acknowledge their kindness and valiant efforts.

Name _____          Date _____

# Self-Evaluation

|                                | Child's Score | | Teacher's Score | |
|--------------------------------|:-----:|:----:|:-----:|:----:|
| I was a good listener.         | Yes   | No   | Yes   | No   |
| I worked quietly.              | Yes   | No   | Yes   | No   |
| I got my work done.            | Yes   | No   | Yes   | No   |
| I was kind to my friends.      | Yes   | No   | Yes   | No   |
| I followed all school rules.   | Yes   | No   | Yes   | No   |
| I was good at _____.  | Yes   | No   | Yes   | No   |
| My day was                     | ☺     | ☹    | 😐    |      |

Teacher's Comments:

_____

_____

_____

_____

_____
Teacher's Signature

_____
Student's Signature

*The Creative K–1 Classroom* © 1999 Creative Teaching Press

# Super Whiz Kid Award

Presented to

_____

for being a good listener, for following directions, and for being helpful and kind to others.

Signed _____

Date _____

whiz Kid

# Whiz Kid Tickets

I'm a Whiz Kid! Ask me why!

Great job, friend!

Thank you for being so thoughtful!

Whiz Kid, Whiz Kid. That's me!

I'm a good friend!

I saw what you did.

Somebody thinks you're special!

Good for you!

*The Creative K–1 Classroom* © 1999 Creative Teaching Press

# ASSESSMENT

This section provides tools for
assessing what students know when they
come to you, what they have learned while being
with you, and in what areas they need more instruction or
practice. These assessments will help you adjust your instruction
to provide appropriate opportunities for all students to grow.

In addition to tools for assessing student abilities, the following pages
describe a method of teaching that uses these assessments to "Teach to Reach
Each," or Prescriptive Teaching. This method applies explicit, systematic instruction
that has been individualized to student needs to accelerate their acquisition of skills.
Instead of "overteaching" skills to students
who already know them, Prescriptive
Teaching methods customize
your instruction to meet
specific student needs.

This section includes the
following assessment tools:

♥ The Seasonal Assessment shows individual student growth over time. (See pages 59–62.)

♥ Authentic Assessment (the systematic sampling of student behavior to see how well and in what ways students are able to do necessary tasks) uses the Skills Inventory. It calls for candidly charting progress toward mastery of end-of-year objectives through informal observation. (See pages 63–68.)

♥ The Phonemic Awareness Inventory assesses students on five levels of phonemic awareness. (See pages 69–73.)

♥ The Sight Words Inventory assesses students' recognition of common sight words. (See page 74.)

♥ The Letter and Sound Identification checklists assess students' recognition of capital and lowercase letters and the sounds they make. (See pages 75–76.)

♥ Use the ABCs and 123s, Self-Portrait, and My Drawings reproducibles to collect samples of penmanship and artwork and record student growth throughout the year. (See pages 77–79.)

♥ The Skills Update informs parents how their child is doing and in what areas he or she needs extra practice. (See pages 80–83.)

## Seasonal Assessments

Take the time at the start of the year to find out what your students already know. Use the Kindergarten Seasonal Assessment (pages 59–60) or First Grade Seasonal Assessment (pages 61–62) as a pre-assessment tool for discovering current ability levels and for ongoing growth throughout the year. Use a different-colored highlighter for each assessment period, marking each item the child has mastered. Be certain to highlight the name of the season with the same-colored highlighter. Each time you assess the child, assess only the skills that were not already mastered the previous quarter. As each task is marked off with a different-colored highlighter, parents will be able to see the learning that has taken place throughout the year.

## Skills Inventory

It is not always necessary to administer a test to know what a child can do. To chart progress toward mastery of end-of-year objectives in an informal way, use the Kindergarten Skills Inventory (pages 63–64) or the First Grade Skills Inventory (pages 65–67). Or, create your own record using the blank skills inventory form on page 68. List your end-of-the-year objectives on the inventory. Be sure to include your state and district standards as well as additional skills you wish your students to master. (We need to teach more than simply what the report card records.) Because most of the objectives are easy to observe during work time, P. E. activities, or whenever students are working independently, you are assessing students in authentic situations, free of anxiety, and measuring actual ability. Carry the inventory on a clipboard. As students work, observe and interact with them, recording your observations on the inventory. The symbols -, ✓, and + make record keeping a snap. Mark a plus for mastery, a check for progress being made, and a minus for not progressing adequately in an area. With only a few pages on a clipboard, you don't have to flip through report cards or individual evaluations to see how a child is doing. This gives you a quick start on Prescriptive Teaching, allowing you to see at a glance who needs work in which areas.

## Phonemic Awareness Inventory

The Phonemic Awareness Inventory (pages 69–73) will help determine where your phonemic awareness instruction should begin and what areas need emphasis. It begins with simple concepts, such as whole word discrimination, and progresses to more complicated concepts, such as phoneme deletion and phoneme substitution. Administer this assessment orally. It requires no reading by the child. It is designed to assess students' awareness of the *sounds* of language, not the *appearance* of language. Choose a different-colored highlighter at each assessment to show progress over time. Be certain to highlight the name of the season with the same-colored highlighter.

## Sight Words Inventory

Administer the Sight Words Inventory (page 74) toward the end of kindergarten to assess word knowledge. Highlight the words students can read or identify. Choose a different-colored highlighter at each assessment to show progress over time. Be certain to highlight the name of the season with the same-colored highlighter.

## Letter and Sound Identification

Each quarter, ask students to name the letters they know on the Letter Identification Checklist (page 75), and highlight each letter the student identifies correctly. Ask students which letter sounds they can recognize on the Sound Identification Checklist (page 76), and highlight each letter they sound correctly. Each quarter, use a different-colored highlighter to show the progression throughout the year. Be certain to highlight the name of the season with the same-colored highlighter.

## Assessment Easy as 123 and ABC

Each quarter, have students write their full name, numbers in sequence, and ABCs on the ABCs and 123s reproducible (page 77). Also, each quarter have students draw a self-portrait on the Self-Portrait reproducible (page 78) and four pictures on the My Drawings reproducible (page 79). File these papers for parent conferences and evaluation time to show the progression of skills throughout the year.

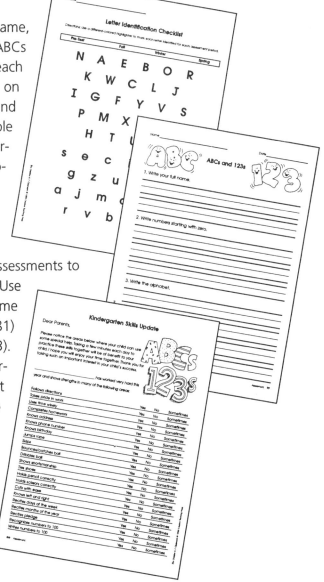

## Skills Update

Before report cards or parent conferences, review your Skills Inventory and Seasonal Assessments to determine areas of need for each student. Use this information to complete and send home the Kindergarten Skills Update (pages 80–81) or the First Grade Skills Update (pages 82–83). This provides valuable information to the parents regarding their child's progress as it relates to grade-level objectives and helps to avoid any surprises at conferences. This also gives the parents an opportunity to work with their child in areas where the student needs practice. Near the end of the year, send home the update and instead of written homework for the rest of the year, ask parents to work on areas where students need extra help.

## Prescriptive Teachers

How can we teach without knowing what our students need to learn? Prescriptive Teaching, or "Teaching to Reach Each," is a method of writing "prescriptions" for individual students. Skills in which students need more practice are recorded on index cards, and explicit instruction is given to those students who need it. By focusing on those skills that students need, you avoid giving "medicine" (or an overdose of teaching) to students who don't need it, and "prescribe" skill practice for the students who do. Students work on their own specific areas of need. In whole-group instruction, individual needs are difficult to address. Some get it, others do not. Without Prescriptive Teaching, which is based on ongoing assessment, many children get lost in the shuffle. Often it is not until the end of the year that the teacher finds out that one student or another does not know a specific concept or skill.

Review the Skills Inventory (pages 63–67), and use one index card for each objective, listing the names of the students who need work on that particular skill, such as identifying a letter or letter sound, recognizing or making rhymes, sequencing, or knowing their phone number or address. The index cards become prescriptions for further need of teaching. Keep the cards in a "Prescriptive Teaching basket" filled with assessment materials such as the following:

- buttons for counting
- rhyming objects
- shoes with laces
- number cards 0–10, 1–100
- alphabet flash cards
- letter-recognition cards
- sequence cards
- pictures of shapes
- crayons
- child scissors
- picture cards
- sight word flash cards
- sound-recognition cards
- jump rope

When students are working independently or with volunteers at centers, choose a skill from the basket to work on, and meet with students either individually or in small groups. Periodically reassess and update the cards. This is also a great resource for parent volunteers who drop in to help. (See Prescriptive Teaching on page 30.) They can take your Prescriptive Teaching basket and work with individual students or small groups without interrupting you or requiring extra effort on your part.

Name _____     Birthday_____

# Kindergarten Seasonal Assessment

Directions: Use a different-colored highlighter to mark mastered tasks for each assessment period.

| Pre-Test | Fall | Winter | Spring |
|---|---|---|---|

Follows directions
Takes pride in work
Uses time wisely
Completes homework
Knows address
Knows phone number
Knows birthday
Jumps rope
Skips
Bounces/catches ball
Dribbles ball
Shows sportsmanship
Ties shoes
Holds pencil correctly
Holds scissors correctly
Cuts with ease
Knows left and right
Recites days of the week
Recites months of the year
Recites pledge
Recognizes numbers to 100
Writes numbers to 100
Sequences numbers
Counts tally marks
Uses tally marks
Creates and interprets simple graphs
Knows <, >, =
Creates simple patterns

Counts to 100 by 1s
Counts to 100 by 10s
Counts to 100 by 5s
Counts to 100 by 2s
Counts sets of objects to 20
Sorts by attribute
Gives reasonable estimates
Adds objects to 10
Subtracts objects from 10
Uses nonstandard units to measure
Recognizes coins
Knows consonant sounds
Knows short vowel sounds
Knows long vowel sounds
Can sequence letters alphabetically
Can create compound words
Decodes CVC words
Segments sounds
Recognizes rhymes
Recognizes main idea
Retells a story in sequence
Communicates thoughts clearly
Demonstrates left to right progression
Puts name on papers
Writes full name
Forms letters correctly
Works well with others

## Recognizes Colors

red        blue        green        yellow        black        white        brown        orange        purple        pink

## Can Read Color Words

red        blue        green        yellow        black        white        brown        orange        purple        pink

The Creative K–1 Classroom © 1999 Creative Teaching Press

Name _____

# Kindergarten Seasonal Assessment

| Pre-Test | Fall | Winter | Spring |
|---|---|---|---|

## Recognizes Shapes

| circle | square | rectangle | triangle | oval |
|---|---|---|---|---|

## Knows Letter Names

| N | O | L | S | P | Z | D | c | o | w | j | x | b |
|---|---|---|---|---|---|---|---|---|---|---|---|---|
| A | R | J | F | M | H | K | i | g | y | m | p | n |
| E | W | I | Y | X | T | s | t | z | k | d | r | q |
| B | C | G | V | Q | U | e | f | u | a | l | v | h |

## Knows Letter Sounds

| m | c | b | d | k | y | w | th | wh | i |
|---|---|---|---|---|---|---|---|---|---|
| s | h | g | j | f | v | z | ch | a | o |
| t | r | n | p | l | x | q | sh | e | u |

## Can Count by Ones to _____

| 5 | 10 | 15 | 20 | 30 | 40 | 50 | 60 | 70 | 80 | 90 | 100 |
|---|---|---|---|---|---|---|---|---|---|---|---|

## Recognizes Numerals

| 0 | 3 | 6 | 9 | 12 | 15 | 18 | 30+ | 60+ | 90+ |
|---|---|---|---|---|---|---|---|---|---|
| 1 | 4 | 7 | 10 | 13 | 16 | 19 | 40+ | 70+ | 100 |
| 2 | 5 | 8 | 11 | 14 | 17 | 20+ | 50+ | 80+ | |

*The Creative K–1 Classroom* © 1999 Creative Teaching Press

Name _____     Birthday _____

# First Grade Seasonal Assessment

Directions: Use a different-colored highlighter to mark mastered tasks for each assessment period.

| Pre-Test | Fall | Winter | Spring |
|---|---|---|---|

Follows oral directions

Takes pride in work

Uses time wisely

Completes homework on time

Knows address

Knows phone number

Knows birthday

Shows sportsmanship

Holds pencil correctly

Knows left and right

Understands calendar concepts

Recites months of the year

Recites pledge

Recognizes numbers to 100

Writes numbers to 100

Sequences numbers

Knows odd and even numbers

Determines missing numbers in equations

Counts tally marks

Creates and interprets simple graphs

Knows <, >, =

Creates patterns

Counts to 100 by 1s

Counts to 100 by 10s

Counts to 100 by 5s

Counts to 100 by 2s

Sorts by attribute

Gives reasonable estimates

Knows subtraction facts 1–20

Knows addition facts 1–20

Demonstrates use of standard measures

Can measure temperature

Uses nonstandard measures

Counts coins

Understands place value to 100s

Tells time by hour and ½ hour

Knows consonant sounds

Knows short vowel sounds

Knows long vowel sounds

Alphabetizes words to second letter

Uses dictionary

Decodes compound words to spell new words

Uses suffixes to make new words

Demonstrates understanding of contractions

Makes rhymes

Segments and blends sounds

Spells high-frequency words

Spells unknown words phonetically

Decodes words phonetically

Reads fluently with expression

Follows written directions

Understands the main idea

Retells stories in sequence

Communicates clearly

Demonstrates left to right progression

Writes fluently

Uses complete sentences

Uses capital letters correctly

Uses correct punctuation (., !, ?)

Uses correct grammar

Writes name on papers

Writes full name

Uses correct penmanship

Works well with others

Name _____

# First Grade Seasonal Assessment

| Pre-Test | Fall | Winter | Spring |
|---|---|---|---|

## Recognizes Shapes

circle    square   rectangle    triangle    oval

## Knows Letter Names

m   c   b   o   i   e   z   W   P   L   D   R   U

u   a   g   j   f   v   q   X   K   Y   N   H   S

s   h   n   p   l   x   Q   V   I   E   G   A   T

t   r   d   k   y   w   Z   J   F   O   B   M   C

## Knows Letter Sounds

m   c   b   d   k   y   w   th   wh   i

s   h   g   j   f   v   z   ch   a   o

t   r   n   p   l   x   q   sh   e   u

## Can Count by Ones to _____

5   10   15   20   30   40   50   60   70   80   90   100

## Recognizes Numerals

0   3   6   9   12   15   18   30+   60+   90+

1   4   7   10   13   16   19   40+   70+   100

2   5   8   11   14   17   20+   50+   80+

*The Creative K-1 Classroom* © 1999 Creative Teaching Press

# Kindergarten Skills Inventory

| | Follows directions | Takes pride in work | Uses time wisely | Completes homework | Knows address | Knows phone number | Knows birthday | Jumps rope | Skips | Bounces/catches ball | Dribbles ball | Shows sportsmanship | Ties shoes | Holds pencil correctly | Holds scissors correctly | Cuts with ease | Knows left and right | Recites days of the week | Recites months of the year | Recites pledge | Recognizes numbers to 100 | Writes numbers to 100 | Sequences numbers | Counts tally marks | Uses tally marks | Knows <, >, = | Creates and interprets simple graphs | Creates simple patterns |
|---|---|---|---|---|---|---|---|---|---|---|---|---|---|---|---|---|---|---|---|---|---|---|---|---|---|---|---|---|
| | | | | | | | | | | | | | | | | | | | | | | | | | | | | |

# Kindergarten Skills Inventory

| | Counts to 100 by 1s | Counts to 100 by 10s | Counts to 100 by 5s | Counts to 100 by 2s | Counts sets of objects to 20 | Sorts by attribute | Gives reasonable estimates | Adds objects to 10 | Subtracts objects from 10 | Uses nonstandard units to measure | Recognizes coins | Knows consonant sounds | Knows short vowel sounds | Knows long vowel sounds | Can sequence letters alphabetically | Can create compound words | Decodes CVC words | Segments sounds | Recognizes rhymes | Recognizes main idea | Retells a story in sequence | Communicates thoughts clearly | Demonstrates left to right progression | Puts name on papers | Writes full name | Forms letters correctly | Works well with others |
|---|---|---|---|---|---|---|---|---|---|---|---|---|---|---|---|---|---|---|---|---|---|---|---|---|---|---|---|
| | | | | | | | | | | | | | | | | | | | | | | | | | | | |

# First Grade Skills Inventory

| | Works well with others | Follows oral directions | Takes pride in work | Uses time wisely | Completes homework on time | Knows address | Knows phone number | Knows birthday | Shows sportsmanship | Holds pencil correctly | Knows left and right | Understands calendar concepts | Recites months of the year | Recites pledge | Recognizes numbers to 100 | Writes numbers to 100 | Sequences numbers | Knows odd and even numbers | Determines missing numbers in equations | Counts tally marks | Creates and interprets simple graphs | Knows <, >, = | Creates patterns | Counts to 100 by 1s | Counts to 100 by 10s | Counts to 100 by 5s | Counts to 100 by 2s |
|---|---|---|---|---|---|---|---|---|---|---|---|---|---|---|---|---|---|---|---|---|---|---|---|---|---|---|---|
| | | | | | | | | | | | | | | | | | | | | | | | | | | | |
| | | | | | | | | | | | | | | | | | | | | | | | | | | | |
| | | | | | | | | | | | | | | | | | | | | | | | | | | | |

# First Grade Skills Inventory

| | Sorts by attribute | Gives reasonable estimates | Knows subtraction facts 1–20 | Knows addition facts 1–20 | Demonstrates use of standard measures | Can measure temperature | Uses nonstandard measures | Counts coins | Understands place value to 100s | Tells time by hour and ½ hour | Knows consonant sounds | Knows short vowel sounds | Knows long vowel sounds | Alphabetizes words to second letter | Uses dictionary | Decodes compound words to spell new words | Uses suffixes to make new words | Demonstrates understanding of contractions | Makes rhymes | Segments and blends sounds | Spells high-frequency words | Spells unknown words phonetically | Decodes words phonetically | Reads fluently with expression | Follows written directions | Understands the main idea | Retells stories in sequence | Communicates clearly |
|---|---|---|---|---|---|---|---|---|---|---|---|---|---|---|---|---|---|---|---|---|---|---|---|---|---|---|---|---|
| | | | | | | | | | | | | | | | | | | | | | | | | | | | | |
| | | | | | | | | | | | | | | | | | | | | | | | | | | | | |
| | | | | | | | | | | | | | | | | | | | | | | | | | | | | |
| | | | | | | | | | | | | | | | | | | | | | | | | | | | | |
| | | | | | | | | | | | | | | | | | | | | | | | | | | | | |
| | | | | | | | | | | | | | | | | | | | | | | | | | | | | |

*The Creative K–1 Classroom* © 1999 Creative Teaching Press

# First Grade Skills Inventory

| | Demonstrates left to right progression | Writes fluently | Uses complete sentences | Uses capital letters correctly | Uses correct punctuation (. , ! ?) | Uses correct grammar | Writes name on papers | Writes full name | Uses correct penmanship |
|---|---|---|---|---|---|---|---|---|---|
| | | | | | | | | | |
| | | | | | | | | | |
| | | | | | | | | | |
| | | | | | | | | | |
| | | | | | | | | | |
| | | | | | | | | | |
| | | | | | | | | | |
| | | | | | | | | | |
| | | | | | | | | | |
| | | | | | | | | | |
| | | | | | | | | | |
| | | | | | | | | | |
| | | | | | | | | | |
| | | | | | | | | | |
| | | | | | | | | | |
| | | | | | | | | | |
| | | | | | | | | | |
| | | | | | | | | | |
| | | | | | | | | | |
| | | | | | | | | | |
| | | | | | | | | | |
| | | | | | | | | | |
| | | | | | | | | | |
| | | | | | | | | | |

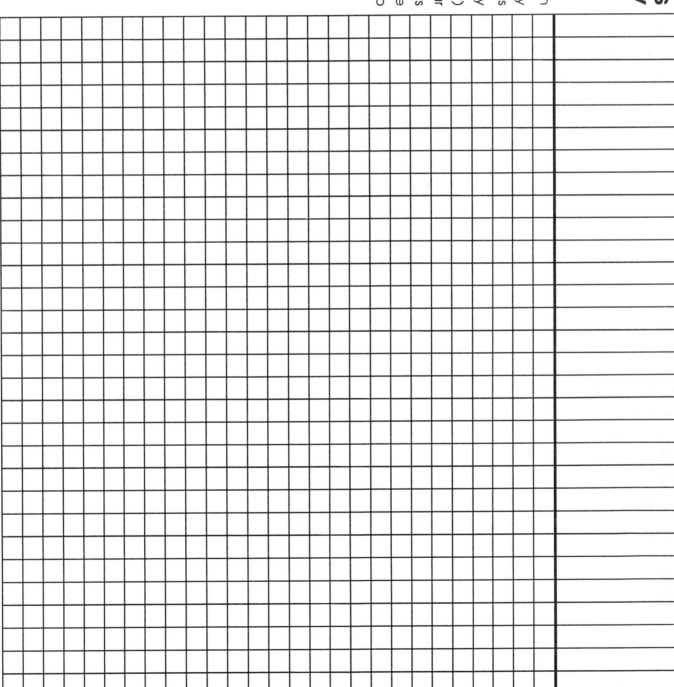

# Phonemic Awareness Inventory

| Pre-Test | Fall | Winter | Spring |
|----------|------|--------|--------|

Directions: Give this inventory orally to each student.
Use a different-colored highlighter to mark mastered tasks for each assessment period.

## LEVEL 1

## Whole Word Discrimination

*Are these words the same?* (Circle words child identifies correctly.)

fat—bat

dip—hip

man—man

red—rid

nut—nut

mat—map

slip—slit

grip—grip

flit—flip

## Rhyming Words—Recognition

*Do these words rhyme?* (Circle words child identifies correctly.)

fun—fan

pig—wig

cheer—year

bread—seed

happy—sappy

girl—boy

sad—mad

sun—fun

play—game

# Phonemic Awareness Inventory

## Rhyming Words—Application

*What word rhymes with _____?*

(Write child's responses on the lines and circle those that are correct.)

man _____     back _____

sit _____      sky _____

eat _____      trip _____

day _____      bump _____

old _____      shell _____

## Sound Matching

*Which word does not belong?* (Circle word child says.)

sun, sad, sip, tub

mat, bat, hop, cat

bee, meat, sea, fee

day, fog, fat, farm

red, bed, mix, sled

## Syllable Counting

*How many syllables do you hear in the word _____?*

(Write child's responses on the lines and circle those that are correct.)

bicycle _____     candlestick _____

garden _____      orangutan _____

opposite _____    crown _____

hippopotamus _____   bedtime _____

*The Creative K–1 Classroom* © 1999 Creative Teaching Press

# Phonemic Awareness Inventory

## LEVEL 2

## Syllable Segmentation
*I'll say a word, then you repeat it slowly.*

(Give examples: *cow-boy, ha-ppy, fu-nny.* Circle words to which child responds correctly.)

rainbow (rain-bow)                color (co-lor)

doughnut (dough-nut)              scissors (sci-ssors)

sidewalk (side-walk)             butterfly (bu-tter-fly)

paper (pa-per)                    umbrella (um-bre-lla)

basket (bas-ket)                  voices (voi-ces)

## Syllable Splitting
*What word do you have when you join these sounds together?*

(Say the onset and then the rime*. Circle words child blends correctly.)

| | | | |
|---|---|---|---|
| j—ump | cl—imb | tr—ain | s—ing |
| t—an | str—eet | cl—ock | p—earl |

* An onset is all the sounds in a word that come before the first vowel. A rime is the first vowel in a word and all the sounds that follow.
(For example, in the word *splash,* the onset is *spl-* and the rime is *-ash.*)

## Phoneme Blending
*Listen and tell me the word I said.*

(*Say each sound slowly.* Circle words child identifies correctly.)

| | | | |
|---|---|---|---|
| n—o | f—a—t | m—o—p | c—a—ke |
| s—ay | s—i—t | w—a—s | w—e—n—t |
| m—e | t—e—n | h—a—ve | s—a—ck |
| r—u—n | c—u—t | s—ai—d | br—o—ke |

*The Creative K–1 Classroom* © 1999 Creative Teaching Press

# Phonemic Awareness Inventory

## LEVEL 3

### Phoneme Approximation

*Do you hear the /b/\* sound at the beginning, middle, or end of _____?*

(Circle words child identifies correctly.)

| | | |
|---|---|---|
| big | tub | crib |
| robot | cabbage | bat |
| banana | grab | table |

\* When letters appear between slash marks (such as /k/), the sound rather than the letter name is represented.

### Phoneme Isolation

*What sound do you hear _____?* (Circle words child identifies correctly.)

| First | Last | In the Middle |
|---|---|---|
| sun | water | feet |
| foot | buff | tub |
| yes | candy | lake |
| red | ten | pan |

## LEVEL 4

### Phoneme Counting

*How many sounds do you hear in these words?*

(Circle words for which child identifies the correct number of sounds. For example, *paint* has four sounds: p-ai-n-t.)

| | | |
|---|---|---|
| at | tent | mom |
| lake | bug | desk |
| paint | hen | up |

*The Creative K–1 Classroom* © 1999 Creative Teaching Press

# Phonemic Awareness Inventory

## Phoneme Segmentation

*Repeat each word slowly so I can hear each separate sound, like c—a—t.*

(Say each word and ask child to repeat it slowly, separating each phoneme. Circle each word child

segments correctly.)

| | | |
|---|---|---|
| me | you | book |
| so | play | skip |
| man | old | scale |

## LEVEL 5

## Phoneme Deletion

*Say the word _____, but leave off the _____.*

(Say each word and ask child to delete beginning or ending sounds. Circle each word to which child

responds correctly.)

| | | |
|---|---|---|
| pop | not | mop |
| can | tab | fin |
| dip | cub | set |

## Phoneme Substitution

*Replace the _____ sound in _____ with _____. What is the new word?*

(Say each word and ask child to substitute the first, middle, or ending sound. Circle words to which child

responds correctly.)

| | | |
|---|---|---|
| pail | log | get |
| cat | tub | pop |
| pig | dice | jump |

Name _____

# Sight Words Inventory

Directions: Use a different-colored highlighter to mark words read for each assessment period.

| Pre-Test | | Fall | Winter | | Spring |
|---|---|---|---|---|---|
| a | come | has | many | school | up |
| about | could | have | me | see | use |
| all | day | he | more | she | very |
| am | did | head | move | so | want |
| an | do | her | my | some | was |
| and | does | here | new | sound | watch |
| are | down | his | no | take | we |
| as | each | how | not | talk | went |
| asked | family | I | now | than | were |
| asks | first | if | of | that | what |
| at | for | in | off | the | when |
| be | from | into | on | their | where |
| because | get | is | once | them | which |
| been | gets | it | one | then | who |
| began | girl | learn | or | there | will |
| blue | go | like | out | they | with |
| but | goes | little | play | thing | words |
| by | going | long | please | this | yellow |
| call | good | look | put | time | yes |
| can | great | made | said | to | you |
| care | had | make | saw | two | your |

*The Creative K–1 Classroom* © 1999 Creative Teaching Press

Name _____

# Letter Identification Checklist

Directions: Use a different-colored highlighter to mark each letter identified for each assessment period.

| Pre-Test | Fall | Winter | Spring |
|----------|------|--------|--------|

N A E B O R

K W C L J

I G F Y V S

P M X Q Z

H T U D

s e c i t f o

g z u w y k

a j m d l x p

r v b n q h

Name _____

# Sound Identification Checklist

Directions: Use a different-colored highlighter to mark each letter sound identified for each assessment period.

| Pre-Test | Fall | Winter | Spring |
|---|---|---|---|

m    s    t    c    h

r    b    g    n    d

j    p    k    f    y

l    v    x    q

w    z

th    ch    sh    wh

i    u    a    o    e

*The Creative K–1 Classroom* © 1999 Creative Teaching Press

Name _____     Date _____

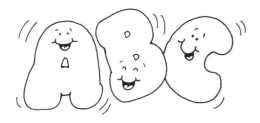   **ABCs and 123s**

1. Write your full name.

_____
- - - - - - - - - - - - - - - - - - - - - - - - - - - - - - - - - - - - - - - - - - - - - - - - -
_____
- - - - - - - - - - - - - - - - - - - - - - - - - - - - - - - - - - - - - - - - - - - - - - - - -
_____

2. Write numbers starting with zero.

_____
- - - - - - - - - - - - - - - - - - - - - - - - - - - - - - - - - - - - - - - - - - - - - - - - -
_____
- - - - - - - - - - - - - - - - - - - - - - - - - - - - - - - - - - - - - - - - - - - - - - - - -
_____
- - - - - - - - - - - - - - - - - - - - - - - - - - - - - - - - - - - - - - - - - - - - - - - - -
_____

3. Write the alphabet.

_____
- - - - - - - - - - - - - - - - - - - - - - - - - - - - - - - - - - - - - - - - - - - - - - - - -
_____
- - - - - - - - - - - - - - - - - - - - - - - - - - - - - - - - - - - - - - - - - - - - - - - - -
_____
- - - - - - - - - - - - - - - - - - - - - - - - - - - - - - - - - - - - - - - - - - - - - - - - -
_____
- - - - - - - - - - - - - - - - - - - - - - - - - - - - - - - - - - - - - - - - - - - - - - - - -
_____

Name _____     Date _____

Here's my self-portrait!

Name _____     Date _____

# My Drawings

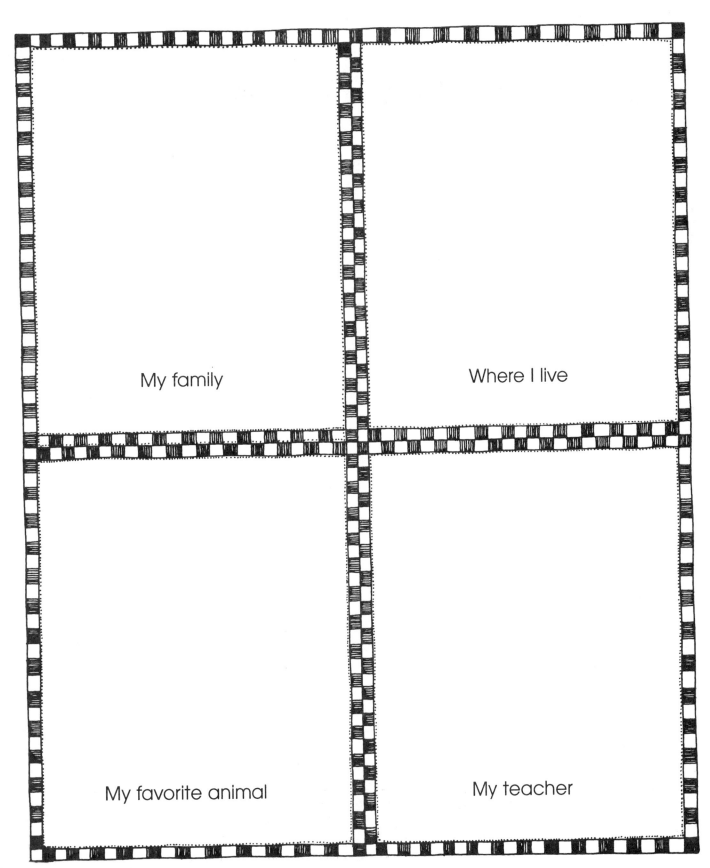

My family

Where I live

My favorite animal

My teacher

# Kindergarten Skills Update

Dear Parents,

Please notice the areas below where your child can use some special help. Taking a few minutes each day to practice these skills together will be of benefit to your child. I hope you will enjoy your time together. Thank you for taking such an important interest in your child's success.

_____ has worked very hard this year and shows strengths in many of the following areas:

| | | | |
|---|---|---|---|
| Follows directions | Yes | No | Sometimes |
| Takes pride in work | Yes | No | Sometimes |
| Uses time wisely | Yes | No | Sometimes |
| Completes homework | Yes | No | Sometimes |
| Knows address | Yes | No | Sometimes |
| Knows phone number | Yes | No | Sometimes |
| Knows birthday | Yes | No | Sometimes |
| Jumps rope | Yes | No | Sometimes |
| Skips | Yes | No | Sometimes |
| Bounces/catches ball | Yes | No | Sometimes |
| Dribbles ball | Yes | No | Sometimes |
| Shows sportsmanship | Yes | No | Sometimes |
| Ties shoes | Yes | No | Sometimes |
| Holds pencil correctly | Yes | No | Sometimes |
| Holds scissors correctly | Yes | No | Sometimes |
| Cuts with ease | Yes | No | Sometimes |
| Knows left and right | Yes | No | Sometimes |
| Recites days of the week | Yes | No | Sometimes |
| Recites months of the year | Yes | No | Sometimes |
| Recites pledge | Yes | No | Sometimes |
| Recognizes numbers to 100 | Yes | No | Sometimes |
| Writes numbers to 100 | Yes | No | Sometimes |

The Creative K–1 Classroom © 1999 Creative Teaching Press

Child's Name _____

| | | | |
|---|---|---|---|
| Sequences numbers | Yes | No | Sometimes |
| Counts tally marks | Yes | No | Sometimes |
| Uses tally marks | Yes | No | Sometimes |
| Creates and interprets simple graphs | Yes | No | Sometimes |
| Knows <, >, = | Yes | No | Sometimes |
| Creates simple patterns | Yes | No | Sometimes |
| Knows geometric shapes | Yes | No | Sometimes |
| Counts to 100 by 1s | Yes | No | Sometimes |
| Counts to 100 by 10s | Yes | No | Sometimes |
| Counts to 100 by 5s | Yes | No | Sometimes |
| Counts to 100 by 2s | Yes | No | Sometimes |
| Counts sets of objects to 20 | Yes | No | Sometimes |
| Sorts by attribute | Yes | No | Sometimes |
| Gives reasonable estimates | Yes | No | Sometimes |
| Adds objects to 10 | Yes | No | Sometimes |
| Subtracts objects from 10 | Yes | No | Sometimes |
| Uses nonstandard units to measure | Yes | No | Sometimes |
| Recognizes coins | Yes | No | Sometimes |
| Knows consonant sounds | Yes | No | Sometimes |
| Knows short vowel sounds | Yes | No | Sometimes |
| Knows long vowel sounds | Yes | No | Sometimes |
| Can sequence letters alphabetically | Yes | No | Sometimes |
| Can create compound words | Yes | No | Sometimes |
| Decodes CVC words | Yes | No | Sometimes |
| Segments sounds | Yes | No | Sometimes |
| Recognizes rhymes | Yes | No | Sometimes |
| Recognizes main idea | Yes | No | Sometimes |
| Retells a story in sequence | Yes | No | Sometimes |
| Communicates thoughts clearly | Yes | No | Sometimes |
| Demonstrates left to right progression | Yes | No | Sometimes |
| Puts name on papers | Yes | No | Sometimes |
| Writes full name | Yes | No | Sometimes |
| Forms letters correctly | Yes | No | Sometimes |
| Other: | Yes | No | Sometimes |

# First Grade Skills Update

## Dear Parents,

Please notice the areas below where your child can use some special help. Taking a few minutes each day to practice these skills together will be of benefit to your child. I hope you will enjoy your time together. Thank you for taking such an important interest in your child's success.

_____ has worked very hard this year and

shows strengths in many of the following areas:

| | | | |
|---|---|---|---|
| Works well with others | Yes | No | Sometimes |
| Follows oral directions | Yes | No | Sometimes |
| Takes pride in work | Yes | No | Sometimes |
| Uses time wisely | Yes | No | Sometimes |
| Completes homework on time | Yes | No | Sometimes |
| Knows address | Yes | No | Sometimes |
| Knows phone number | Yes | No | Sometimes |
| Knows birthday | Yes | No | Sometimes |
| Shows sportsmanship | Yes | No | Sometimes |
| Holds pencil correctly | Yes | No | Sometimes |
| Knows left and right | Yes | No | Sometimes |
| Understands calendar concepts | Yes | No | Sometimes |
| Recites months of the year | Yes | No | Sometimes |
| Recites pledge | Yes | No | Sometimes |
| Recognizes numbers to 100 | Yes | No | Sometimes |
| Writes numbers to 100 | Yes | No | Sometimes |
| Sequences numbers | Yes | No | Sometimes |
| Knows odd and even numbers | Yes | No | Sometimes |
| Determines missing numbers in equations | Yes | No | Sometimes |
| Counts tally marks | Yes | No | Sometimes |
| Creates and interprets simple graphs | Yes | No | Sometimes |
| Knows <, >, = | Yes | No | Sometimes |
| Creates patterns | Yes | No | Sometimes |
| Counts to 100 by 1s | Yes | No | Sometimes |
| Counts to 100 by 10s | Yes | No | Sometimes |
| Counts to 100 by 5s | Yes | No | Sometimes |
| Counts to 100 by 2s | Yes | No | Sometimes |
| Sorts by attribute | Yes | No | Sometimes |

*The Creative K–1 Classroom* © 1999 Creative Teaching Press

Child's Name _____

| | | | |
|---|---|---|---|
| Gives reasonable estimates | Yes | No | Sometimes |
| Knows subtraction facts 1–20 | Yes | No | Sometimes |
| Knows addition facts 1–20 | Yes | No | Sometimes |
| Demonstrates use of standard measures | Yes | No | Sometimes |
| Can measure temperature | Yes | No | Sometimes |
| Uses nonstandard measures | Yes | No | Sometimes |
| Counts coins | Yes | No | Sometimes |
| Understands place value to 100s | Yes | No | Sometimes |
| Tells time by hour and ½ hour | Yes | No | Sometimes |
| Knows consonant sounds | Yes | No | Sometimes |
| Knows short vowel sounds | Yes | No | Sometimes |
| Knows long vowel sounds | Yes | No | Sometimes |
| Alphabetizes words to second letter | Yes | No | Sometimes |
| Uses dictionary | Yes | No | Sometimes |
| Decodes compound words to spell new words | Yes | No | Sometimes |
| Uses suffixes to make new words | Yes | No | Sometimes |
| Demonstrates understanding of contractions | Yes | No | Sometimes |
| Makes rhymes | Yes | No | Sometimes |
| Segments and blends sounds | Yes | No | Sometimes |
| Spells high-frequency words | Yes | No | Sometimes |
| Spells unknown words phonetically | Yes | No | Sometimes |
| Decodes words phonetically | Yes | No | Sometimes |
| Reads fluently with expression | Yes | No | Sometimes |
| Follows written directions | Yes | No | Sometimes |
| Understands the main idea | Yes | No | Sometimes |
| Retells stories in sequence | Yes | No | Sometimes |
| Communicates clearly | Yes | No | Sometimes |
| Demonstrates left to right progression | Yes | No | Sometimes |
| Writes fluently | Yes | No | Sometimes |
| Uses complete sentences | Yes | No | Sometimes |
| Uses capital letters correctly | Yes | No | Sometimes |
| Uses correct punctuation (., !, ?) | Yes | No | Sometimes |
| Uses correct grammar | Yes | No | Sometimes |
| Writes name on papers | Yes | No | Sometimes |
| Writes full name | Yes | No | Sometimes |
| Uses correct penmanship | Yes | No | Sometimes |

# MAKING HOMEWORK A HABIT

Yes, there is homework in kinder-garten and first grade! Kindergarten is the perfect time to begin the "homework habit." Students are generally so excited about going to school, that having homework seems like a rite of passage. Capitalize on this excitement. Teach them from the start the importance of being responsible, of returning assignments, and of taking pride in work well done. Not only will homework reinforce the concepts covered at school, but it will instill in your students an important sense of responsibility and a marvelous sense of pride and accomplishment.

Homework can be handled in many ways. Some families are eager for academic "brain strain." Others appreciate concept reinforcement. The primary focus of Making Homework a Habit is to build bridges between family and school, giving students an opportunity to "show off their smarts" at home and to provide hands-on "happy time" for parent and child. Use and adapt the fol-lowing suggestions to fit your situation. It is not necessary to do everything. Often, less is better. Be discriminating and do what works best for you.

## Homework Notes

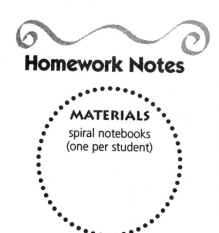

**MATERIALS**
spiral notebooks
(one per student)

Record sight words, spelling words, vocabulary, math problems, or other skills that students need to work on in their own spiral notebook. Each student's notebook will have different homework according to which skills they need to practice. Have students take home their spiral notebook every day for parents to check each night and return it daily to school. Invite parents to make comments or send you notes relating to other subjects in the notebook. Be sure to respond quickly to each note.

## Sharing

### MATERIALS
items to share

Sharing in front of a group is an important part of oral-language development. Children need many opportunities to talk. Assigning each child a "sharing day" is one way of ensuring that students have this opportunity. At the beginning of the year, group students into four "working" groups: groups of students with mixed abilities who get along well with each other. Assign each group a color and a sharing day. For example, the red group might share on Monday, the blue group on Tuesday, etc. Friday can be used for anyone's sharing day, or as a make-up day for students who were absent. Set your standard at the beginning of the year. Decide whether you will allow toys to come to school; if it will become a bragging time; if objects to share must relate to the week's theme; if items must be photographs, handmade objects, artwork, or from nature. Encourage families to participate in the planning of sharing time by having them prepare for it with their child. Encourage students to share books and items relating to the season or the current thematic unit. Use these items as a springboard for concept-related discussion.

## Class Pet

### MATERIALS
Traveltime reproducible
(page 92)
stuffed animal
doll clothes
small suitcase or duffel
journal

Though bears are popular and easy to come by, any stuffed animal will do for this activity, and having two "pets" will increase the opportunities students have to take them home. An animal that can wear doll clothes is particularly fun. Each animal will need a small suitcase or duffel and a journal. Attach a copy of the Traveltime reproducible to the front flap of the journal so any questions parents might have can be easily answered. Send the pet home with a student at your discretion to be returned to class the next day. Invite students to write with their parents a description of the adventures they had with the class pet. Have students share their journal entries during sharing time.

# Kindergarten Book Buddies

Organize your paperback books into groups of five to six books. Include in each group very simple, moderately simple, and read-aloud books. Mark these books with a sticker to differentiate them from books students have at home. Color-code the stickers according to difficulty level. For example, level one (red stickers) are short vowel decodable books; level 2 (green stickers) are long vowel decodable books; level 3 (blue stickers) are a mix of long and short vowels, are decodable, and have only a few sentences on a page; level 4 (yellow stickers) have more words on a page and are more difficult; and level 5 (orange stickers) are beginning chapter books. Place each group of books into a freezer storage bag, and number the bags with a marker. Have at least ten more bags of books than you have students in class. There will be times when you will need them to fill in for bags that have not been returned. Follow the directions below to implement a book buddy program with your students.

1. Attach a reading log to each student's homework folder. Students should bring this folder to school each day and take it home each night.
2. Each kindergarten student takes home a different "book buddy bag" on Monday of each week.
3. Ask parents of kindergarten students to read to their child each night.
4. Have parents mark the reading log with one tally mark for each 20 minutes of reading.
5. Ask parents to total the number of tally marks at the end of the week and remind their child to return the books to class by Friday.
6. As books are returned, the bags are arranged in sequence in a book buddy storage box or container.
7. On the following Monday, give each student the next numbered bag of books to take home. For example, give the student who took bag #10 last week, #11 the following week. If that student failed to return bag #11, new books would not be checked out to him or her. An extra bag of books would be substituted in the place of #11 for the receiving student to avoid throwing off everyone's order of books. The following week, when the book bag is returned, students continue taking book bags in numbered sequence.

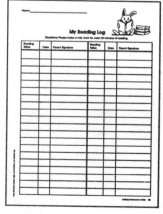

## First Grade Home Reading

### MATERIALS

My Reading Log (page 93)

Comprehension Questions
(pages 94–95)

Home Reading Coupons
(page 96)

paperback books

variety of colored stickers

scissors

homework folders

Organize your books into different levels of difficulty as described in Kindergarten Book Buddies (see page 86). Assign each student a colored level of books to take home according to your assessments. Have students choose three books at a time to take home, only selecting from the books with the colored stickers on the spine that match their level. Photocopy the Comprehension Questions, cut each section apart, and send one or two sections home with students when they check out books. Ask parents to review the questions orally with their child to help stimulate conversation about and comprehension of the book. Send home with students Home Reading Coupons for parents to fill out on each book. These will let you know if and when the student should be given a higher level of books. Permit students to return the books as frequently as they wish and take home new books just as quickly. Follow the directions below to implement a book buddy program with your students.

1. Attach a reading log to each child's homework folder. Students should bring this folder to school each day and take it home each night.
2. Each first grade student takes three books home at a time and can check out more as soon as the first three are returned.
3. Have parents of first grade students listen to their child read each night.
4. Ask parents to orally review some of the comprehension questions with their child and complete a Home Reading Coupon.
5. Have parents mark the reading log with one tally mark for each 20 minutes of reading rather than for each book read to equalize the playing field as far as readability of·books goes and so as not to punish students who read longer books.
6. Ask parents to total the number of tally marks at the end of the week.

## Homework in a Box

Though this program does require storage space, the benefits are immensely rewarding. You will need at least one old lunch box per student, plus several extras. Use art supplies to decorate and number each box. Photocopy the activity letters (written to parents) on the following pages. Place the letter and related materials for each activity in a box. The activities should alternate between math, thinking, and language-arts activities. Give each student a box on Monday, and ask that it be returned before Friday. Only send home one box per week with each student. Use the Homework Box Sign-out Chart to record the comings and goings of each box. Mark the date of departure for each box, and cross off the date when the box is returned. If you keep the boxes coming and going in numerical order, it will eliminate a multitude of potential problems. Have a parent volunteer check the contents of each box before sending it home with another student.

## High Card Wins

Use the following activity to introduce students to the concept of less than, greater than, and equal to. This is an easy and fun way for students to practice number-value skills with their family. Place a deck of cards and the following letter in a lunch box, and send it home with a student.

Dear Parents,

Please read the following instructions to play High Card Wins with your child.

1. Divide the deck of cards into two equal piles.
2. Each player turns over one card.
3. The player with the highest number takes both cards.
4. When both players draw the same card, "War" begins. Each player then lays two cards facedown on top of his or her first card. A third card is played faceup. Again, the player with the highest card takes all the cards.
5. When all cards are played, players recycle their winnings and continue to play until one player has all the cards.

## Sequence Stories

In advance, write out simple, familiar stories on index cards. Divide each story into about five main parts, each written on a separate card for students to sequence. Include simple drawings above the text, or photocopy illustrations from the storybook and glue them on the cards. Place each story's cards in a separate resealable plastic bag. Place several bags in a lunch box with crayons or markers, paper, and the following letter.

### MATERIALS

familiar storybooks
index cards
glue (optional)
resealable plastic bags
crayons or markers
paper

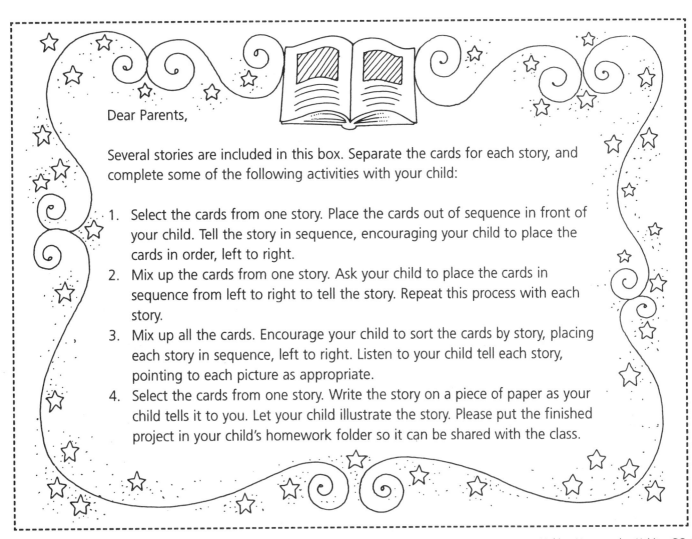

Dear Parents,

Several stories are included in this box. Separate the cards for each story, and complete some of the following activities with your child:

1. Select the cards from one story. Place the cards out of sequence in front of your child. Tell the story in sequence, encouraging your child to place the cards in order, left to right.

2. Mix up the cards from one story. Ask your child to place the cards in sequence from left to right to tell the story. Repeat this process with each story.

3. Mix up all the cards. Encourage your child to sort the cards by story, placing each story in sequence, left to right. Listen to your child tell each story, pointing to each picture as appropriate.

4. Select the cards from one story. Write the story on a piece of paper as your child tells it to you. Let your child illustrate the story. Please put the finished project in your child's homework folder so it can be shared with the class.

## Book of Surprises

**MATERIALS**

Surprise reproducible
(page 98)

bookbinding materials

markers

Make enough copies of the Surprise reproducible for each student to have one copy. Create a Book of Surprises by folding the pages in half lengthwise and binding them into a book on the left side (i.e., the side with the loose edges). Create a Surprise Box by decorating a lunch box with question marks. Place a copy of the letter (below), markers, and the Book of Surprises in the lunch box for students to take home. After each student has contributed to the Book of Surprises, invite students to share their clues with the class and ask them to guess the item.

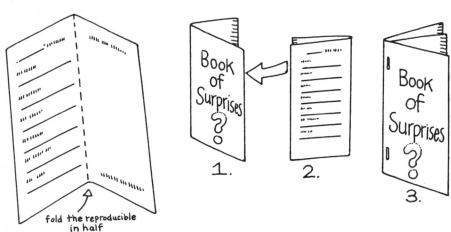

fold the reproducible
in half

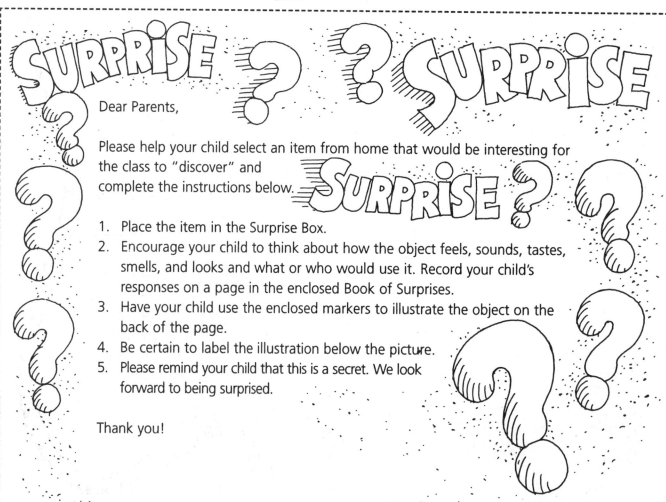

Dear Parents,

Please help your child select an item from home that would be interesting for the class to "discover" and complete the instructions below.

1. Place the item in the Surprise Box.
2. Encourage your child to think about how the object feels, sounds, tastes, smells, and looks and what or who would use it. Record your child's responses on a page in the enclosed Book of Surprises.
3. Have your child use the enclosed markers to illustrate the object on the back of the page.
4. Be certain to label the illustration below the picture.
5. Please remind your child that this is a secret. We look forward to being surprised.

Thank you!

## Jump Rope Rhymes

**MATERIALS**
long jump rope
short jump rope
book of jump rope rhymes

Place a long and short jump rope in a lunch box. Include a book of jump rope rhymes, such as *Anna Banana* by Joanna Cole, and the following letter. Send the box home with students.

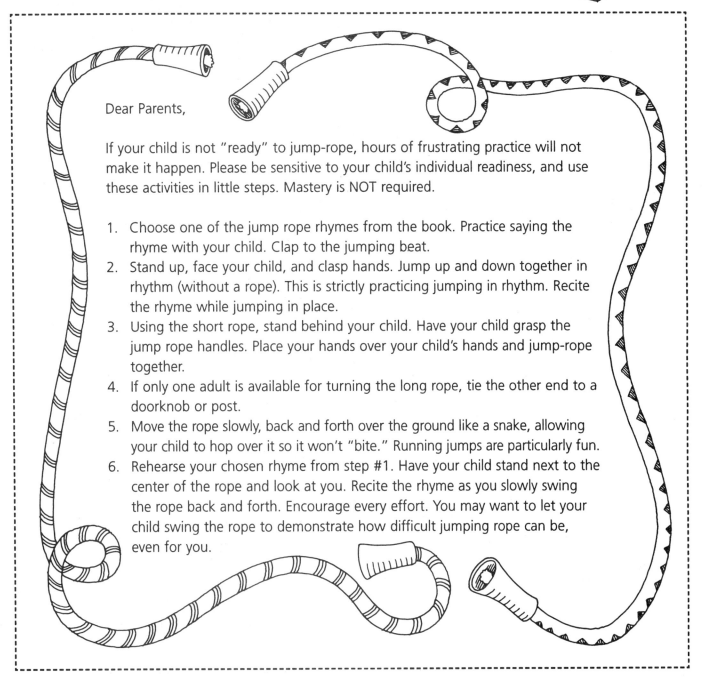

Dear Parents,

If your child is not "ready" to jump-rope, hours of frustrating practice will not make it happen. Please be sensitive to your child's individual readiness, and use these activities in little steps. Mastery is NOT required.

1. Choose one of the jump rope rhymes from the book. Practice saying the rhyme with your child. Clap to the jumping beat.
2. Stand up, face your child, and clasp hands. Jump up and down together in rhythm (without a rope). This is strictly practicing jumping in rhythm. Recite the rhyme while jumping in place.
3. Using the short rope, stand behind your child. Have your child grasp the jump rope handles. Place your hands over your child's hands and jump-rope together.
4. If only one adult is available for turning the long rope, tie the other end to a doorknob or post.
5. Move the rope slowly, back and forth over the ground like a snake, allowing your child to hop over it so it won't "bite." Running jumps are particularly fun.
6. Rehearse your chosen rhyme from step #1. Have your child stand next to the center of the rope and look at you. Recite the rhyme as you slowly swing the rope back and forth. Encourage every effort. You may want to let your child swing the rope to demonstrate how difficult jumping rope can be, even for you.

# Traveltime

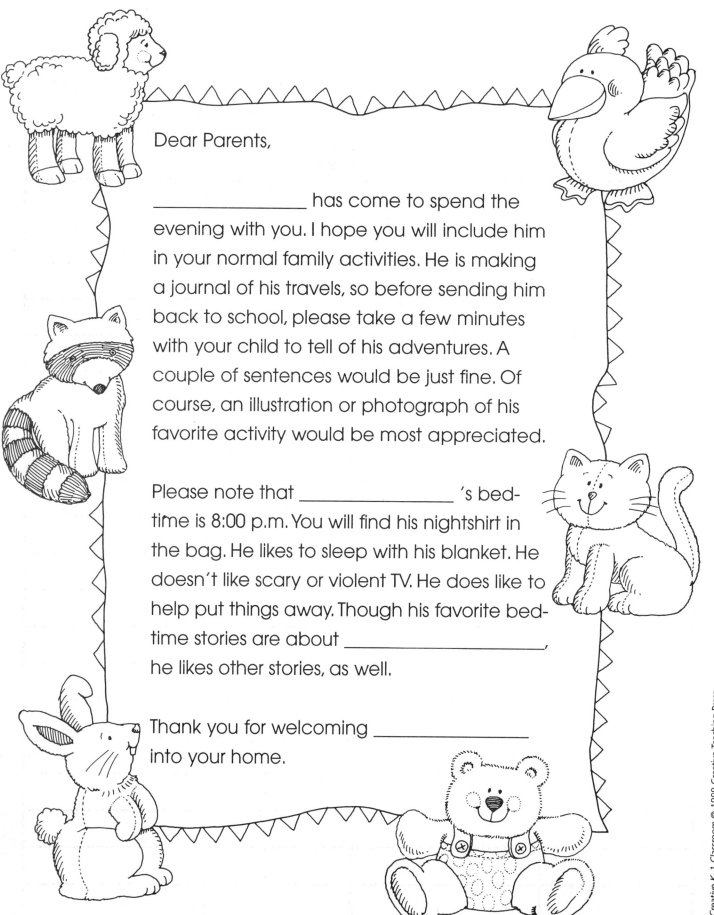

Dear Parents,

_____ has come to spend the evening with you. I hope you will include him in your normal family activities. He is making a journal of his travels, so before sending him back to school, please take a few minutes with your child to tell of his adventures. A couple of sentences would be just fine. Of course, an illustration or photograph of his favorite activity would be most appreciated.

Please note that _____ 's bedtime is 8:00 p.m. You will find his nightshirt in the bag. He likes to sleep with his blanket. He doesn't like scary or violent TV. He does like to help put things away. Though his favorite bedtime stories are about _____, he likes other stories, as well.

Thank you for welcoming _____ into your home.

Name _____

# My Reading Log

Directions: Please make a tally mark for each 20 minutes of reading.

| Reading Tallies | Date | Parent Signature | Reading Tallies | Date | Parent Signature |
|---|---|---|---|---|---|
| | | | | | |
| | | | | | |
| | | | | | |
| | | | | | |
| | | | | | |
| | | | | | |
| | | | | | |
| | | | | | |
| | | | | | |
| | | | | | |
| | | | | | |
| | | | | | |
| | | | | | |
| | | | | | |
| | | | | | |
| | | | | | |
| | | | | | |
| | | | | | |
| | | | | | |

## Comprehension Questions #1

1. Describe the main character.
2. What was the problem?
3. How did the character deal with the problem?
4. Tell about three events that happened in the story.
5. Should the character have done something differently? What? Why?

## Comprehension Questions #2

1. Where did this story take place?
2. What happened there?
3. Who was involved?
4. What is another way the story could have ended?
5. Is there a lesson to learn in this story? What is it?

## Comprehension Questions #3

1. What was the problem in this story?
2. What happened? Why?
3. How was the problem solved?
4. What else could have happened?
5. What would you have done?

## Comprehension Questions #4

1. What was your favorite part of the story? Why?
2. Have you ever read another story that is similar to this? How were they the same? How were they different?
3. How would you change the main character?
4. How are you like that character? How are you different?
5. What could be another name for this story?

## Comprehension Questions #5

1. Describe the main character.
2. What was his or her problem?
3. What did he or she do about it?
4. Did he or she make the right decision? Explain.
5. How did the story end?

## Comprehension Questions #6

1. What was this story about?
2. What did the main character want?
3. What happened?
4. Then what?
5. How would you like the story to be different?
6. Did this story really happen?

*The Creative K–1 Classroom* © 1999 Creative Teaching Press

## Comprehension Questions #7

1. Did this story really happen?
2. Who was the main character?
3. How did the story end?
4. Describe a new way to end the story.
5. What could be another name for this story?

## Comprehension Questions #8

1. Describe the main character.
2. How is this character like you?
3. Tell about three events in the story.
4. How did the story end?
5. What would you have done if you were in this story?

## Comprehension Questions #9

1. Is this story fiction or nonfiction?
2. What was the book about?
3. What was your favorite part?
4. What did you learn from this book?

## Comprehension Questions #10

1. What did you learn by reading this book?
2. What did you think was interesting about _____?
3. What are three facts from the book?
4. What information was important in the book? Is it a fact or an opinion?

## Comprehension Questions #11

1. What questions do you have after reading the book?
2. What does the book remind you of?
3. Tell how the subject relates to other books you've read.
4. What would happen if _____?
5. Tell an opinion from the book. Tell a fact.

## Comprehension Questions #12

1. Who? (Who is the book about, or what is the topic of the book?)
2. What? (What did the subject do, or what's important about it?)
3. Where? (Where does it live, or where did the event take place?)
4. When? (When did this happen?)
5. Why? (Why is this important to know, or why did the event occur?)
6. How? (How did this happen, or how does this relate to other things?)

# Home Reading Coupons

Date _____

_____ has read _____
(name) (book title)

to me_____ times. The book was
(number)

_____ too easy.

_____ too difficult.

_____ just right.

_____ a challenge at first, but we mastered it.

Comprehension:

_____ excellent    _____ fair    _____ needs some work

Words we are still having difficulty with:

_____

- - - - - - - - - - - - - - - - - - - - - - - - - - - - - - - - - - - - - -

Date _____

_____ has read _____
(name) (book title)

to me_____ times. The book was
(number)

_____ too easy.

_____ too difficult.

_____ just right.

_____ a challenge at first, but we mastered it.

Comprehension:

_____ excellent    _____ fair    _____ needs some work

Words we are still having difficulty with:

_____

*The Creative K–1 Classroom* © 1999 Creative Teaching Press

# Homework Box Sign-out Chart

| Homework Box Number | Name | Date |
|---|---|---|
|  |  |  |
|  |  |  |
|  |  |  |
|  |  |  |
|  |  |  |
|  |  |  |
|  |  |  |
|  |  |  |
|  |  |  |
|  |  |  |
|  |  |  |
|  |  |  |
|  |  |  |
|  |  |  |
|  |  |  |
|  |  |  |
|  |  |  |
|  |  |  |

_____'s Surprise
(name)

Here it is!

It feels

_____.

It sounds

_____.

It tastes

_____.

It smells

_____.

It looks

_____.

It reminds me of

_____.

Here's one more clue:

_____.

What is it?

A picture of my surprise!

*The Creative K–1 Classroom* © 1999 Creative Teaching Press

# STUDENT SPOTLIGHT

Student Spotlight activities are designed to honor each student,

celebrate student birthdays, and give students an opportunity to share with the class

a brief report about a hero during the given spotlight week. Record student names the week of,

or near, their birthday on your School Calendar (see page 5) at the beginning of the year. (Honor students

who have summer birthdays with an "un-birthday" at a prescheduled time during the year.) Each family will

know at the start of the year their child's spotlight week and, if you use thematic units, the theme being

studied. Thus, if a child is scheduled months ahead for a spotlight celebration during a week of a the-

matic unit on Hawaii, the family can plan a theme-related spotlight. The birthday snack could

become the cooking experience and might consist of making fruit kabobs or

rolling bananas in chocolate and nuts.

## Spotlight Week

**MATERIALS**

Spotlight Celebration letter (page 101)

Spotlight Announcement letter (page 102)

Send home the Spotlight Celebration letter at the beginning of the school year to inform parents about their child's special week. Schedule the birthday celebration for the Friday of the student's spotlight week. Invite the family to plan a 20-minute family activity honoring the birthday (or un-birthday) child of the week. The student could dance, sing, or play the piano; relatives with special talents could be invited to share; a family skit, video, or art project would also be appropriate. Whatever is offered, big or small, make a big to-do about the student. On Monday of the spotlight week, invite parents to help their child decorate a bulletin board with items that are of special interest to him or her. Instead of bringing a birthday snack, encourage the spotlight family to bring necessary items for the students to create or cook their own snack. Or they may bring a snack. However, have them check with you beforehand to help coordinate the snack with your theme or to check for appropriateness. Discourage cookies, cupcakes, and ice cream. Request that parents not send birthday invitations to school. Nothing hurts more than being left out. Make a list of students' names, addresses, and phone numbers (after receiving approval from parents) so parents may make arrangements outside of school. Send home the Spotlight Announcement letter a few weeks before the student's spotlight as a reminder.

## Hero Report

**MATERIALS**

Heroes reproducible (page 103)

My Research Project reproducible (page 104)

During each student's spotlight week, he or she will have an opportunity to share about a hero. Have students prepare a simple oral report and turn in a written report. Even kindergartners can do a research report. They can copy one to three sentences and draw a picture. First graders can do the report with a cover page, a bibliography, and three to five sentences. Send home the Heroes reproducible with both first grade and kindergarten students early in the year so students have plenty of time to prepare. Try to include that hero in the week's lesson

My Research Report
Abe Lincoln
by Cameron

to enhance the experience. Or, schedule which heroes to include in reports based on the season. For example, students can report on Martin Luther King, Jr., and Rosa Parks in January; Abraham Lincoln, George Washington, and Ben Franklin in February; Thomas Jefferson in September for Constitution Week; John Smith in November; or Thomas Edison during a thematic unit on electricity. You can schedule one hero each week throughout the year. Send home the My Research Project reproducible to first grade students. Have students present their hero report on Friday of their spotlight week. Kindergarten students do not have the same requirements, so you may want to adapt your own letter for them.

# Spotlight Celebration

## Dear Parents,

Every child is an important person. Spotlighting children in a special way during the year is one way of emphasizing to themselves and their friends that they are valued. Though a child's spotlight may be scheduled at any time during the year, I have tried to schedule it during the week of his or her birthday. For each child who has a summer birthday, an "un-birthday" celebration will be planned.

_____'s spotlight has been tentatively scheduled for the week of _____. Before this time, you may want to plan appropriate activities to celebrate your child and family. For example, your child might like to dance, sing, or play the piano. Relatives with special talents could be invited to share. A family skit, video, or art project would also be appropriate. Whatever is offered, big or small, a big to-do will be made about your child. Please clear all plans with me, however, in advance.

### Bulletin Board
Each child has the opportunity to decorate his or her own bulletin board for the spotlight week. Pictures, awards, special treasures . . . anything that represents the child and is of special interest to him or her can be displayed. Please plan on preparing the bulletin board Monday morning before school and removing all items by Friday afternoon.

### Snack
Birthday snacks have been a long-time tradition. In our class, however, if you would like to bring a snack, please choose something nutritious, such as vegetables with dip, celery with peanut butter, yogurt, or fruit kabobs. If you would like to prepare a snack with the class, please discuss it with me first. If a snack is not convenient for you, just let me know. I do not want this to be a burden for you.

### Report
Another aspect of the spotlight is the hero report. Each student will prepare a simple report relating to a hero. The report is outlined in detail on the page entitled My Research Project. The report will be presented Friday morning as part of your child's celebration.

Thanks for helping to make this week special for your child!

# Spotlight Announcement

Dear Parents,

_____'s spotlight is coming up the week of _____.
The theme we will be studying that week will be
_____. You may decorate your child's bulletin board Monday morning with anything that is special to your child. It will be ready to take down on Friday.

A report on a hero, including a title page, three to five sentences of information, and a picture, drawing, or object relating to the week's theme should be prepared as part of the Friday presentation. Your child will be asked to discuss it briefly with the class.

Each child's family is encouraged to visit with the class on the Friday morning of the spotlight week. A presentation that includes home videos, baby books, a family talent . . . something that spotlights the importance of your child to the family is highly encouraged.

The schedule for Friday's spotlight is as follows:
_____ child/family presentation
_____ teacher presentation
_____ snack

Instead of the traditional birthday goodies, please bring to school only nutritious snacks for the spotlight celebration. Vegetables with dip, fruit kabobs, yogurt, etc. would be welcome and highly appropriate. If this is not convenient for you, just let me know. I don't want this to be a burden for you.

It's going to be a fun, fun day, so don't forget to bring your camera. Let's get together and discuss your plans. I'm happy to help in any way.

# Heroes

Choose one of the suggested heroes on the list or one of your own.

### American Presidents
Andrew Jackson
Thomas Jefferson
Abraham Lincoln
Teddy Roosevelt
George Washington

### Outstanding Individuals
Ludwig van Beethoven
Helen Keller
Wilma Rudolph
Joni Erickson Tada
Stevie Wonder

### Science & Medicine
Marie Curie
Steven Hawking
Florence Nightingale
Jonas Salk
Albert Schweitzer
Leonardo da Vinci

### Inventors
Alexander Graham Bell
Louis Braille
George Washington Carver
Thomas Edison
Henry Ford
Benjamin Franklin
Samuel Morse
Sequoyah
Eli Whitney
Wright Brothers

### Pioneers
Daniel Boone
Davy Crockett
Louis and Clark
Sacajawea
John Smith

### Patriots
Nathan Hale
Patrick Henry
Francis Scott Key
Molly Pitcher
Betsy Ross
Haym Salomon
Sons of Liberty
Uncle Sam

### Naturalists
Johnny Appleseed
   (John Chapman)
John James Audubon
John Muir

### Peacemakers
Mohandas K. Gandhi
Nelson Mandela
Mother Teresa

### Civil Rights Leaders
Susan B. Anthony
Martin Luther King, Jr.
Rosa Parks
Tecumseh
Harriet Tubman

### Famous Authors
Hans Christian Andersen
Maya Angelou
Roald Dahl
Langston Hughes
A. A. Milne
Dr. Seuss
Mark Twain

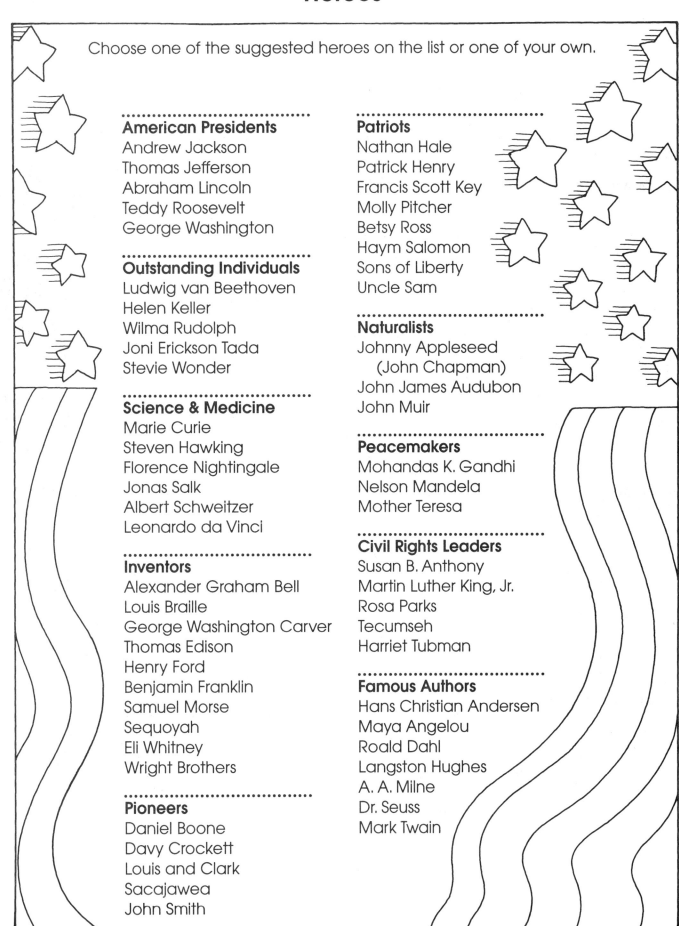

Name _____

# My Research Project

Due date: _____

Selected topic:

_____

## Content
Questions to be answered in the report:
1. When?
2. Where?
3. Who?
4. What happened?
5. What was the problem?
6. How was the problem resolved?
7. Why is this person considered a hero?
8. How can I be a hero?

## Format
All projects should meet the following guidelines:
1. The topic should represent a heroic person.
2. Use a minimum of two printed resources.
3. Write a minimum of three to five sentences.
4. Report should be printed (by child) and include a title page and a simple bibliography.
5. Include a minimum of one illustration.
6. This information page must appear at the end of the report.

## Presentation
1. Though the report must be hand printed, the child will not read the report. Instead, it will be reported orally in front of the class. Please practice with your child before the event for proper oral presentation technique.
2. Artifacts, visitors, and other related enrichment and/or activities are encouraged.

# PHONICS AND PHONEMIC FUN

Phonemic awareness is the ability to recognize and manipulate individual sound units (phonemes) in spoken language: to examine language independent of meaning, to see relationships between sounds in words, and to rearrange sounds to create new words. For example, the word *chick* is made up of three phonemes (/ch/ /i/ /k/); it can be changed to the word *pick* by replacing /ch/ with /p/. Use the activities in this section to allow students to experience the joy of language while mastering important pre-reading skills, such as rhyming; alliteration; and the isolation, segmentation, blending, and manipulation of sounds.

## Clap a Rhyme

MATERIALS
sentence strips
markers
pocket chart

Write a familiar rhyming poem on sentence strips, writing the rhyming words with a different-colored marker. Place the sentence strips in a pocket chart. Say the poem with the class, clapping when you come to the colored words. Do not say the rhyming word aloud. Ask students what rhyming word would fit into the poem. Substitute different rhyming words for the colored words. Talk with students about what makes the words rhyme. Place the sentence strips at a learning center for additional practice.

## Rhymes to Recess

Give each student a Rhyming Words Picture Card. Brainstorm a few rhyming words with the class as a review. Ask students to think of a word (or words) that rhymes with their picture as a "ticket" to recess.

## Ah, Shucks

In advance, make a copy of the Syllable Picture Cards for every two students and cut them apart. Divide the class into pairs, and give each student six picture cards. Ask students to mix up their cards and place them facedown in a pile. Have partners sit facing each other and simultaneously turn over their top card and count the number of syllables in their picture word. The student with the most syllables takes both cards. When each student's card has the same number of syllables, students turn over another card. The student who has the card with the highest number of syllables takes all the visible cards. Play continues until one student has all the cards.

## Hum Dee Dum Dum

Photocopy a set of the Syllable Picture Cards, and cut them apart. Display each picture to the class. Have students say the word while clapping each syllable. Then, invite students to hum the word while clapping each syllable. Students will be able to count the number of syllables more accurately when they hum the words because the sounds break naturally between each syllable. Store the cards at a learning center for independent practice.

## Syllable Sort

**MATERIALS**

Syllable Picture Cards (page 116) or name cards

index cards

pocket chart

Number five index cards, and display them across the top row of a pocket chart. Distribute a Syllable Picture Card or name card to several students. Invite students to place their card under the number that corresponds to the number of syllables in their picture word or name. Invite the class to clap out the number of syllables in each word as you say it together. Write the number of syllables on the back side of each card so students can self-check their answers at a center.

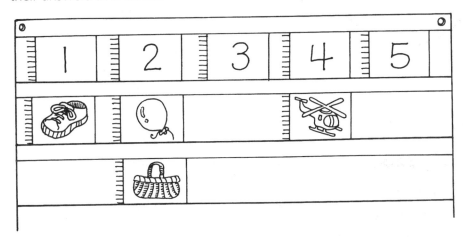

## Alliterative Sentences

**MATERIALS**

sentence strips

pocket chart

Wikki Stix or colored markers

glue

construction paper

crayons or markers

bookbinding materials

Brainstorm with the class alliterative sentences, such as *Brainy Brian blows blue bubbles, Linda loves lemons,* or *Trenton told a tale.* Write the alliterative sentences on sentence strips, and place them in a pocket chart. Invite students to identify the beginning sounds of alliterative words and place Wikki Stix (or circle with a marker) around the initial sound. Glue the sentence strips to construction paper, and invite students to illustrate each sentence. Bind pages into an alliterative class book. Place the class book at a learning center for additional practice and enjoyment.

## I Know Some Words

**MATERIALS**

"I Know Some Words" song

pictures of objects (optional)

Teach the song "I Know Some Words" to your students. Invite students to name words that start with the given sound at the end of the song. You may want to provide a picture clue if the students need help thinking of words that begin with the given sound. Sing the song again using different beginning sounds.

♫ **I Know Some Words**
*(sing to the tune of "Here We Go Around the Mulberry Bush")*

I know some words that start with /s/,
Start with /s/, start with /s/.
I know some words that start with /s/,
I bet that you do, too.

*Silly, sister, snake*

## Charlie Runs 'Round the Sun

**MATERIALS**

"Charlie Runs 'Round the Sun" rhyme

Chant the rhyme "Charlie Runs 'Round the Sun," substituting a student's name for *Charlie.* Have that student name words that begin with the chosen sound or letter. This activity can also be done using the ending sound of a word. Repeat the song with a different student's name and a different sound.

 **Charlie Runs 'Round the Sun**

Charlie runs 'round the sun.
Charlie runs 'round the moon.
Charlie knows words that start with /m/
On this very afternoon. /m/ /m/ /m/.

*Mom, money, monkey*

## Counting Sounds

### MATERIALS
individual chalkboards
or scrap paper

Some words have a different number of letters than sounds. For example, *pill* has four letters but only three sounds (/p/ /i/ /l/), and *ape* has three letters but only two sounds (/a/ /p/). Slowly say aloud words that can be easily segmented into separate sounds. Ask each student to make a tally mark on an individual chalkboard or on scrap paper for each sound heard. Then, invite students to hold up the appropriate number of fingers when asked how many sounds they heard in the word. Repeat the sounds of each word as needed to ensure each student's understanding.

## Slow-Talking Mama

### MATERIALS
none

Isolate the individual phonemes or the onsets and rimes in students' names to give them an assignment or dismiss them from class. For example, say /s/ /i/ /d/ or *st–acy*. Tell the class a "secret message" in the same manner.

## It Sounds Like

### MATERIALS
none

Make a list of rhyming word pairs. Using a rap-like rhythm, chant the following: *It sounds like* _____ *but it starts with* _____. Insert one word from the rhyming word pair in the first blank and the first letter of the second word in the second blank. Then, repeat the first word twice, and have students respond with the new word. For example, *It sounds like <u>bed</u> but it starts with <u>/r/</u>. Bed, bed, red.* Or, *It sounds like <u>jam</u> but it starts with <u>/h/</u>. Jam, jam, ham.*

## Same Sound

Invite a student to tell something he or she did before coming to school. Substitute the first letter of the student's name to begin every word in the sentence. For example, *Johnny ate toast* becomes *Johnny jate joast.* As students become more proficient in substituting sounds, invite them to substitute the first letter of each word. For added fun, choose a sound to begin each student's name and call each student with the substituted sound for the remainder of the day (e.g., Bennifer, Bendy, and Bristine).

## Blend and Say

Refer to the list of rimes and onsets on page 111 to make words. Whisper a rime to one student and an appropriate onset to another student. Encourage the students as they each say their sounds to the class. Ask the class to repeat the sounds in a chant-like manner, faster and faster, finally blending the sounds to form the new word. Once the class has figured out the word, invite them to chant the following rhyme, using the given onset and rhyme.

*Sp   ill, sp   ill.*
*Put them together and what do you say?*
*Spill, spill.*
*Hip, hip, hooray!*

## Flower Power

### MATERIALS

Flower Spinner reproducible (page 117)

tagboard or card stock

scissors

brass fasteners

In advance, copy the Flower Spinner reproducible, trace it onto tagboard or cardstock, and cut it out. Trace and cut out the smaller circle. Use the lists of onsets and rimes as reference to write a rime on the smaller circle and several onsets on the larger flower or to write an onset on the smaller circle and several rimes around the larger flower. Rotate the larger flower as you write each onset or rime so the two word parts will align right side up. Use a brass fastener to attach the small circle to the front of the larger flower. Invite students to spin the flower and blend the onsets and rimes to practice making and saying words.

### Rimes and Onsets

| | | | | | |
|---|---|---|---|---|---|
| -ad | d, f, gl, m, r, s | -en | d, h, m, p, t, wh | -ob | b, c, j, m, r, s |
| -ag | b, h, r, s, t, w | -id | b, d, gr, h, k, l | -og | cl, d, f, fr, h, l |
| -an | c, m, p, r, t, v | -ig | b, d, f, p, tw, w | -op | c, fl, h, m, p, t |
| -ap | c, fl, g, l, m, n | -ill | b, f, h, m, p, w | -ot | c, d, g, h, n, p |
| -at | c, h, m, p, r, s | -in | f, p, s, t, tw, w | -ug | b, d, h, l, m, r |
| -ed | b, f, l, r, sl, w | -ip | d, fl, h, l, r, s | -un | b, f, n, r, s, sh |
| -ell | b, f, s, t, w, y | -it | b, f, h, l, p, s | | |

### Onsets and Rimes

| | | | | |
|---|---|---|---|---|
| ch | -at, -ill, -in, -ip, -op, -ug | sh | -ed, -ell, -in, -op, -ot, -un |
| cl | -am, -an, -ap, -ip, -og, -op | st | -ar, -ep, -ill, -ing, -op, -un |
| fl | -ag, -ap, -at, -ip, -it, -op | th | -an, -at, -en, -in, -is, -ug |

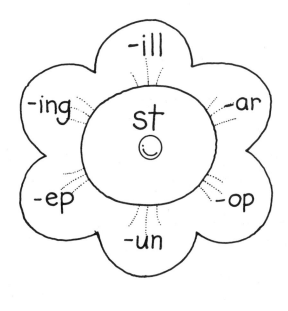

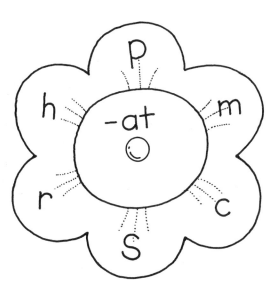

## Make a Word

Ask each student to choose nine of the short vowel word families on the bottom of the Bingo reproducible and cut them out. Have students glue one word family to each space on their bingo card. When all students have finished preparing their card, call out different consonants. Ask students to write each consonant in one of the spaces to make a word. They may write the same consonant on more than one square. Continue playing until a student has made at least one word for each square on one column or row and calls *Bingo*. Invite students to read aloud their words.

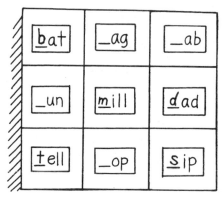

## What's My Rule?

Write CVC words (i.e., three-letter words that follow the consonant/vowel/consonant pattern) on individual index cards. Have students work at a learning center to analyze and sort the words by self-selected attributes. Possible categories might include same initial or ending consonant, same vowel, or same rime family. A student does not need to read each card to have success with this activity. As a student becomes more proficient with decoding skills, however, words can be sorted by meaning.

## Vowel Chant

Photocopy the Vowel Poems, and enlarge them or write them on chart paper. Chant the rhymes with your students to reinforce short and long vowel sounds.

I

I is for inchworm and igloo,
For itch, and for ink.
It's also for ice cream and iron,
And icicle, I think.
ih – ih– I

Short A

A says /a/ quite often.
/a/ is a lovely sound.
It's used in words like apple,
And these others we have found:

(List other short a words.)

# Rhyming Words Picture Cards

# Rhyming Words Picture Cards

# Rhyming Words Picture Cards

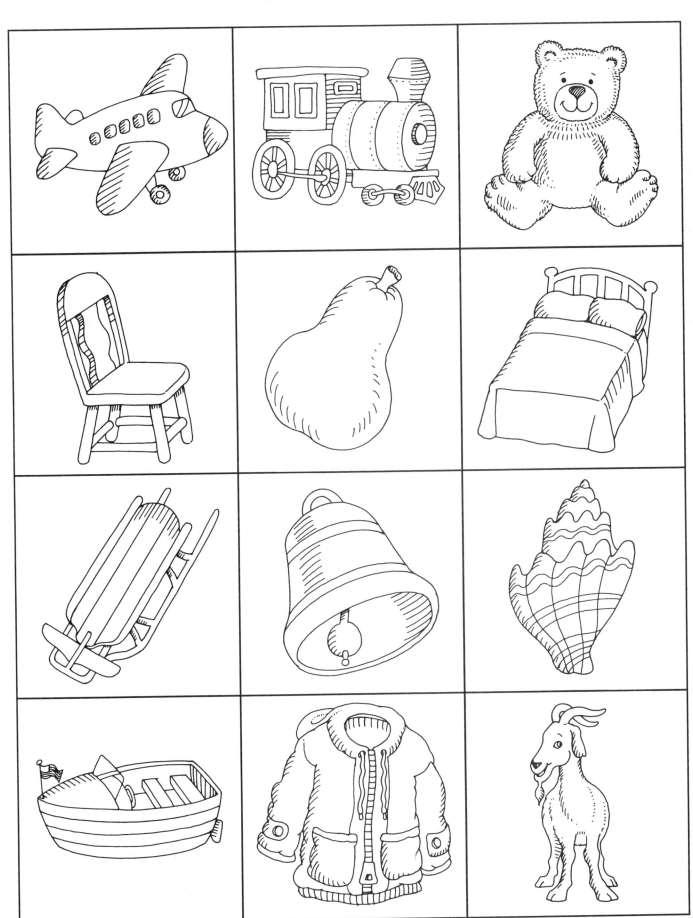

# Syllable Picture Cards

*The Creative K–1 Classroom* © 1999 Creative Teaching Press

# Flower Spinner

# Bingo

| | | |
|---|---|---|
| | | |
| | | |
| | | |

| | | | | |
|---|---|---|---|---|
| ___ab | ___an | ___ell | ___ill | ___og |
| ___ack | ___ap | ___en | ___in | ___op |
| ___ad | ___at | ___id | ___ip | ___ug |
| ___ag | ___ed | ___ig | ___it | ___un |

# Vowel Poems

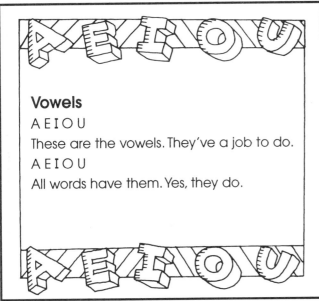

**Vowels**

A E I O U

These are the vowels. They've a job to do.

A E I O U

All words have them. Yes, they do.

**I**

I is for inchworm and igloo,
For itch, and for ink.
It's also for ice cream and iron,
And icicle, I think.
ih – ih– I

**Short A**

A says /a/ quite often.
/a/ is a lovely sound.
It's used in words like apple,
And these others we have found:

*(List other short a words.)*

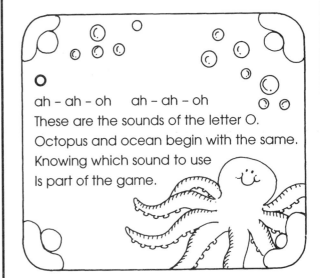

**O**

ah – ah – oh    ah – ah – oh
These are the sounds of the letter O.
Octopus and ocean begin with the same.
Knowing which sound to use
Is part of the game.

**E**

eh – eh – ee    eh – eh – ee
If it doesn't say eh,
It might say ee.
Give it a try
And you will see.

**U**

*(Recite this poem to a rap beat.)*

U is for umbrella and unicorn.
The sound is not always uniform.
You hear it in fun and also in tune.
You hear it in sunny and the month of June.
uh – oo – U!

# SHARED READING

Conducted as a whole-group, small-group, or one-on-one activity, shared reading involves students reading from an enlarged text (e.g., overhead transparency, large-print chart, big book, or sentence strips in a pocket chart) in unison with the teacher. Have students read aloud everything they can and listen to text they do not recognize without drawing attention to themselves. Lead students to make predictions about the story, identify familiar words and phrases, recognize new words and phrases, and read character names.

Introduce text by pointing out features such as the title, author, illustrator, and illustration style. Have students make predictions about the text by answering open-ended questions such as *What do you think this book will be about? Where will it take place? Who are the characters?* and *Is it fact or fiction?* Depending on the skills emphasized, you may discuss the title page; the page count; and features of print such as indented lines, capital letters, and punctuation.

The first time through a book, have students listen silently while you track each word with a decorated pointer to draw attention to the print and model concepts of print such as left-to-right progression and return sweep. After students hear the text several times, have them join in whenever they are comfortable. They may even use the pointer to lead the group. As they become acquainted with the text, have students read all predictable or familiar text without the support of your voice. When finished with a story, invite students to discuss what they learned, liked, and disliked, and any general thoughts they had.

## Reading Circle

**MATERIALS**
Reading Circle chart
(page 124)

It is important to expose students to a variety of writing genres. Copy the Reading Circle chart, and keep track of the kinds of books you read in class by making a tally mark in the appropriate space. Refer to the chart often to determine as a class what type of book to read next and to practice counting by fives.

# Story Map

## MATERIALS

Story Map reproducible
(page 125)

Summary Map reproducible
(page 126)

overhead transparency and
projector or chart paper

Copy the Story Map or Summary Map reproducible onto an overhead transparency or chart paper. Fill it out while reading to help improve student comprehension and to review the parts of a story. Do not limit questions to literal questions to which the answer has been directly stated. Instead, encourage higher-level thinking skills by asking open-ended questions as well.

Ask the following questions to complete the Story Map:
- What is the title?
- Who is the author?
- Who is the illustrator?
- Who are the main characters of the story?
- Where does the story take place?
- What is the problem?
- How is the problem solved?
- What is your favorite part?

Ask the following questions to complete the Summary Map:
- How does the story begin?
- List three events from the story.
- How does the story end?

Ask the following questions to develop higher-level thinking skills:
- What does the story remind you of?
- How is it like another story we have read?
- What is your favorite part?
- Why do you think it ended the way it did?
- How else could it have ended?

## Compare and Contrast

### MATERIALS
2 jump ropes or hula hoops

sentence strips

After reading two books on a similar subject or that have similar elements, use jump ropes or hula hoops to create a Venn diagram on the floor. Write the book titles on separate sentence strips, and place them above each circle. Ask students how the books are alike. Write their comments on sentence strips, and invite students to place the strips where the two circles overlap. Record student comments on how each story is different, and invite students to place each strip under the proper heading.

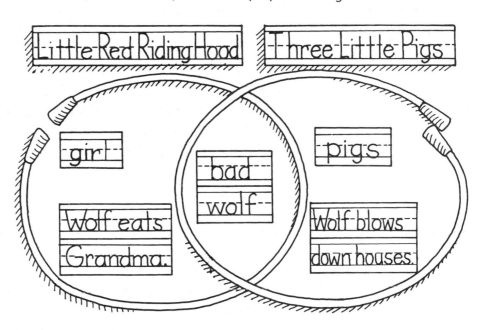

## Choral Reading

### MATERIALS
predictable story or poem

sentence strips

pocket chart

pointer

Select a short section of repetitive text from a predictable story or poem, such as *Run, run as fast as you can. You can't catch me, I'm the Gingerbread Man.* Write the text on sentence strips, and place them in a pocket chart. Read aloud the story or poem. Each time you get to the repetitive text, invite a student to point to the words as the class reads them aloud.

## Detective Eyes

**MATERIALS**

chart paper or sentence strips

toilet-paper tubes (optional)

sticky notes

As you review text on chart paper or sentence strips, invite your students to put on their "detective eyes" and hold their hands to their eyes as if looking through binoculars. Or, have students use toilet-paper tubes as binoculars. Ask students to examine the text as a detective and share what they notice about it. Demonstrate how print works by modeling your observations, drawing attention to the number of words in a sentence, and showing how a sentence does not necessarily end at the end of a line. Draw attention to the space between each word. Change the meaning of the text by writing new words on sticky notes and placing the notes over the original words. Discuss with students how we read from top to bottom and from left to right.

## Concept Books

**MATERIALS**

paper

crayons or markers

bookbinding materials

This activity will help familiarize students with print as they reinforce their understanding of thematic concepts. Type on separate pages one or two simple sentences about a major concept from your thematic unit. Leave sufficient space on each page for an illustration. (Only cover one concept each day.) Each day give each student one copy of a page. Ask students to read and reread each sentence while pointing to the words. As each new concept is added, review the previous pages to reinforce print and concept understanding. Photocopy the pages, and bind them into individual student books. Allow students time to illustrate each page to personalize their book and add to its meaning.

## Book of Important Words

**MATERIALS**

computer

paper

crayons or markers

bookbinding materials

Select words from class reading to include in vocabulary instruction. Discuss the words, and have the class help develop definitions for them while you model writing them in front of the class. Print the definitions on the computer, and use them to create a class book titled *Our Book of Important Words*. Invite each student to illustrate a word, and record the student's name on the page. Use the book in a variety of ways throughout the year. Read a definition (or have a student read it), and have the class guess the vocabulary word. Or, read a vocabulary word, and have students respond with its definition. Challenge students to use the word correctly in a sentence. Make the book available for reference and pleasure.

# Reading Circle

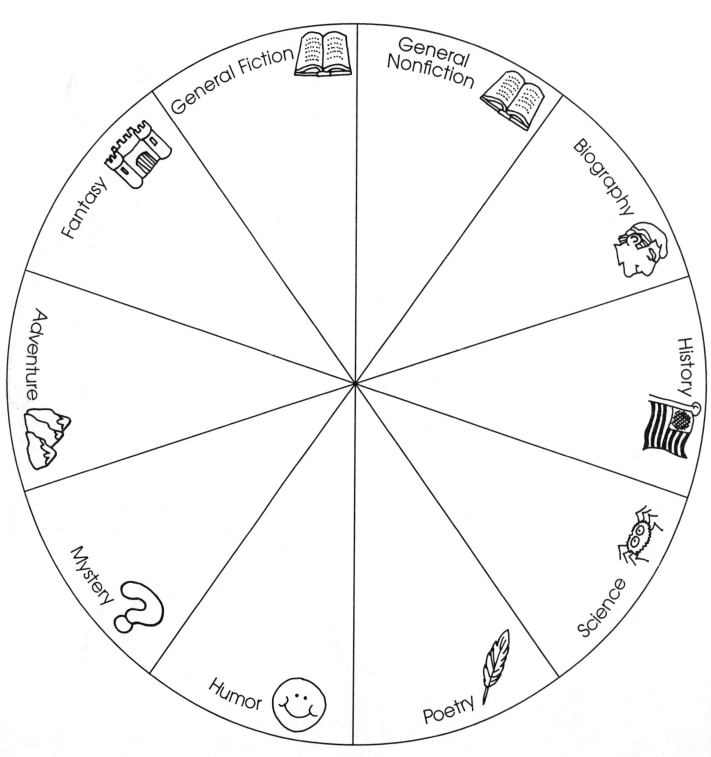

*The Creative K–1 Classroom* © 1999 Creative Teaching Press

# Story Map

Title

Illustrator

Author

Problem

Characters

Favorite Part

Solution

Setting

# Summary Map

| Beginning |
| --- |
|  |

| Event 1 |
| --- |
|  |

| Event 2 |
| --- |
|  |

| Event 3 |
| --- |
|  |

| Ending |
| --- |
|  |

# GUIDED READING

Guided reading is generally a more formal, instructional reading activity conducted one-on-one or with small, ability-level groups. Each student in a group uses the same short text, taking turns reading independently as the teacher and other group members provide support. A guided-reading group works with a story for several days, rereading it each day with different goals in mind, including fluency, expression, comprehension, sight word identification, and practice with phonics concepts. Time between readings is spent extending the story through drama, art, writing, and other reading activities.

Students' first experiences with guided reading should be based on shared-reading texts or simple, familiar stories. Introduce a guided-reading book in the same way as a shared-reading book—with predictions and a discussion of the book's features and specific concepts of print. Then, have students scan the book to become familiar with its vocabulary and identify potentially problematic words. Students' first experience with the body of the story may involve "real" reading of the text or simply "telling" the story based on recognized words and picture clues. As students work through and reread the story, provide decoding strategies, support, and discussion topics. At the conclusion of the story, have students discuss new words they learned, their opinions of the story, and general thoughts they had.

## Say It like the Character

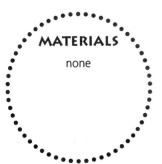

MATERIALS

Have students read a passage silently. Then, ask students to silently reread it as they think the character might make it sound. Ask students to read it aloud, saying the text as they think the character would. Ask students what emotions they were trying to express while reading. Point out different types of print, such as italic or bold, and discuss how these features are reminders of how we can use our voices when reading.

## Super Reader Hat

**MATERIALS**

large construction paper

stapler

Wrap a large sheet of construction paper into a cone shape, staple it closed, and label it *Super Reader Hat*. During guided reading, allow each reader to wear the hat and pass it to the next reader when finished.

## Thumbs Up!

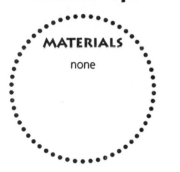

**MATERIALS**

While students follow along during guided reading, have them put their thumbs up when they hear a certain sight word or letter sound. This will help students stay focused during the reading even when it is not their turn.

## Mr. Microphone

**MATERIALS**

Styrofoam ball

cellophane paper or plastic wrap

toilet-paper tube

glue

Wrap a Styrofoam ball with cellophane paper or plastic wrap, and glue it to a toilet-paper tube to make a "microphone." As each student reads during guided reading, pass the microphone to the reader. Students will look forward to having their turn when they have a microphone to read into.

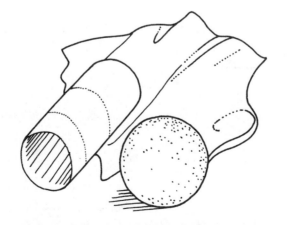

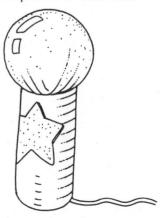

## Eye Spy

### MATERIALS

wiggly eyes
glue
craft sticks

Have each student glue a wiggly eye to a craft stick. Have students use their craft stick as a bookmark while following along during guided reading. Ask students to locate a given word or sound with their "Eye Spy" stick.

## Word Frames

### MATERIALS

construction-paper bookmarks
scissors

In advance, cut a rectangular hole in the center of a construction-paper bookmark for each student. As students read during guided reading, have them "frame" certain words with their word-frame bookmark. This is especially helpful for breaking a big word into smaller parts. For example, have students frame only the root word and then slide the frame over to add the suffix.

## Searching for Signals

### MATERIALS

chart paper or big books

Select sentences from reading books that correspond to specific punctuation marks that you want to teach students. Write the sentences on chart paper or use big books to show examples. Tell students to listen and decide which reading gives the best idea about the character or event. Read the passage twice; once in a monotone voice, and the other using all the punctuation marks. Ask students which was more interesting. Point out the punctuation marks, and tell students to be on the lookout for them in their reading.

# INDEPENDENT READING

Independent reading involves students not only reading books, but using all the written materials in the classroom, including wall charts and environmental print. Independent reading promotes fluency and challenges students to become independent problem solvers. During independent reading, students can read on their own or with partners. By having students read quietly but not silently, you can monitor student reading and they can hear their own reading to help them determine if their reading makes sense. Have students choose their books from book baskets that are arranged by genre, level, or class-made books.

Students must learn to differentiate words from letters and to track left to right and top to bottom. Though watching you point to words in a big book models appropriate behavior, it is not enough to prepare a student for independent reading. Individual practice is the only way to make this skill automatic.

## Mini-Books

**MATERIALS**
storybook
smaller versions of story

After several shared-reading experiences with the same book, create smaller versions of the same story. Mini-books are easily made using a greeting card format on computer publishing programs. Invite students to point to each word as they read the books themselves or take them home to share with their family members.

## Read the Room

MATERIALS

pointer sticks

Students look forward to a 15-minute period of independent reading when they have a large number of "can-do" opportunities in the room. Pair students to give them an opportunity to share with, encourage, and reinforce each other as they take turns pointing and reading to each other. Have students use pointer sticks to track words as they walk around the room reading everything displayed on charts or walls. Have students look for familiar words, rhyming words, spaces between words, capital letters, and punctuation. Include a large variety of reading material for a print-rich room. The items listed below can all be used during Read the Room time.

phonemic charts                     names
sentence strips                       number charts
vocabulary murals                   nursery rhyme charts
song charts                            word wall
class-made books                    lists
posters                                  pocket charts
alphabet charts                       story maps
labels                                    menus
storybook boxes                      interactive writings
color words                            leveled books
Book of Important Words (page 123)

## Storybook Boxes

MATERIALS

small boxes

Have students create a storybook box for the books they make, and encourage them to read their books again and again. Give each student a small box. The grocery store is the perfect place to find little boxes, and baby-food jars come in boxes that are just the right size. Have students take their box home to decorate with their families. Have students keep it in their desk or on a separate shelf. Primarily, the books kept here are small versions of class big books so students know them very well. Invite students to read and reread the familiar stories in their box and share them with friends for a Literacy Center activity, or invite students to read the stories alone or with a partner during Read the Room (see above). If older students visit your room, invite your students to read the stories to their buddies.

## Vocabulary Mural

**MATERIALS**

butcher paper
student artwork
markers
sentence strips

Use students' artwork to create a thematic bulletin board. Display students' artwork on a large piece of butcher paper. Have each student use a marker to label on sentence strips each part of the mural with appropriate vocabulary. Have students refer to the mural when writing to include "big words" or to check for spelling. Use the mural to play games, such as asking students to find a word on the mural that rhymes with *mouse* or *toast*. Write another set of words that match for independent-reading activities and word sorts. Invite students to refer to the words on the mural during Read the Room (see page 131) or writing activities.

## Matchups

**MATERIALS**

empty cereal box
scissors
file folder
envelope
glue

Cut out the cover picture from an empty cereal box, and divide it into twelve rectangular sections. Write on the back of each section something for students to match, such as uppercase letters. Then, divide the inside of a file folder into twelve sections. Write a matching lowercase letter in each section so that if you place the cereal-box pieces over the file folder, the correct letters will match. Glue an envelope to the inside front cover. Cut apart the sections of the cereal box, and place the pieces in the envelope. Have students match the pieces to the file folder so they can check their own work by revealing the cereal-box cover. These independent-learning activities can be made to give students practice matching letters (uppercase to lowercase), sounds to letters, words to pictures, and sentences to pictures. They are self-checking and help to reinforce concepts without direct instruction.

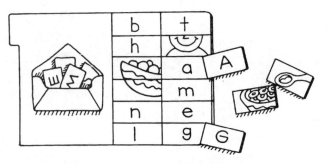

# Rebus Sentence Strips

**MATERIALS**

colored sentence strips

pictures of objects and places from old catalogs, magazines, stickers, or phonics worksheets

glue

pocket chart

Write several copies of each of the frames below on separate sentence strips. Make each set on the same-colored sentence strips. Write the set number on the back side in the upper right-hand corner for easy identification and sorting. Glue a catalog or magazine picture, a sticker, or a picture from an old phonics worksheet in each blank. Write ending punctuation marks on separate sentence strips. Have students work with a partner to mix and match the sentence parts to make new sentences. Invite one student to form a sentence in a pocket chart, and have the partner read it. Then, have them trade roles. As students improve in their skills, have them progress from the first set to sets two through five. Students may want to use the first sets with the later ones to increase their choices. Create additional sets by adding a few new words and phrases to the sets.

**Set #1**

| | |
|---|---|
| I see | a _____ |
| Can I see | the _____ |

**Set #2**

| | |
|---|---|
| Is a _____ | in the _____ |
| A _____ is | on the _____ |
| The _____ is | |

**Set #3**

| | |
|---|---|
| Is the _____ | on the _____ |
| The _____ will go | in the _____ |
| A _____ will go | into the _____ |
| My _____ is | |
| Is my _____ | |

**Set #4**

| | |
|---|---|
| He will sit _____ | at the _____ |
| We will sit _____ | in the _____ |
| She will not hop | up the _____ |
| I will go | on the _____ |
| His _____ is | |
| Will it fit | |
| It will fit | |

**Set #5**

| | |
|---|---|
| No, she will not run | up the _____ |
| Yes, I will run | in the _____ |
| Yes, she ran | on the _____ |
| No, you will nap | |
| No, he fell | |

# Nursery Rhyme Puzzle

## MATERIALS
index cards
stickers or colored markers
rubber band
nursery rhymes

Write each word of a familiar nursery rhyme on a separate index card. Place a sticker or draw a colored dot on the back side of each card to color-code each rhyme. Write the title of the rhyme on an index card to place on top of the pile. Secure the cards with a rubber band. Have students sequence the cards on the floor. Have them refer to the capital letters as clues to what word begins the line. Even before being independent readers, students can often sequence the cards by looking at the first or last letter, the capitalization and punctuation, word patterns, and the length and shape of the words. When they finish, ask students to point to each word while reading it aloud. Have students self-check the rhyme by comparing it to a printed copy of the rhyme.

# Read and Match

## MATERIALS
small objects or pictures
cardboard or card stock
glue
index cards

Prepare this activity by gluing small objects to sturdy pieces of cardboard. Write the name of each object on the back of the cardboard. Make a matching set of index cards with the words written on them, one card for each object. Have students read the word cards and match them to the objects. After they have matched each card, they may turn over the object to check their work. If objects are not available, glue pictures to card stock.

# PRINTING

Learning to print is a powerful means of developing letter-recognition skills. It also enables the beginning writer to create stories with greater confidence and less effort. There is a place in the word-study curriculum for short, directed attention to handwriting. Practicing efficient movements in handwriting helps students feel the way a letter is formed. It helps fix the letter features in the student's mind and visual memory, increasing automaticity. When writing becomes automatic, it becomes more fluent and is produced with less effort. Attention to helping students acquire smooth, efficient movements in handwriting is essential. Writing must be legible, organized in lines with space, and produced with some fluency. Use the following suggestions to promote printing skills:

♥ Let students watch you write. They will observe that you write in one direction and that you leave spaces between words.

♥ Make the letter in the air.

♥ Make the letter on the table.

♥ Make the letter in large form on chart paper or a Magna Doodle®.

♥ Brainstorm words that start with this letter so students have an association of letters and sounds.

♥ In a student handwriting book, write a letter at the beginning of a line so the student has a clear model and knows how to practice that letter.

♥ Teach similar letters together.

♥ Provide daily, supervised practice.

♥ Provide reference models.

## Touch and Learn

### MATERIALS
play dough
airtight container

Students will enjoy penmanship practice when you allow them to touch and feel what they are doing. Give each student a small amount of play dough. Write a letter on the board, and discuss how the letter is formed. Invite students to use their dough to form the letter. Have students feel the shape of their letter and display it on their desk. Collect the dough, and store it in an airtight container at a learning center for students to use with other letters.

## One-Step Circle

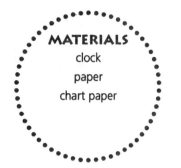

### MATERIALS
clock

paper

chart paper

To properly make several letters, students need to start at the top of a line and travel counterclockwise to make a circle. Show students where to begin to make a "one-step" circle. Show students the "one" position on a clock. Tell them they will begin their one-step circle at the one position, just to the right of the twelve. Tell students to travel counterclockwise to make a circle. This becomes the beginning shape for the letters *a, c, d, g, o,* and *q.* Giving the correct stroke a name helps to differentiate it from the backwards, or "bottom-up," circles. Invite students to practice making one-step circles into letters as volunteers draw them on chart paper.

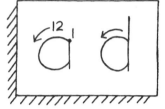

## Squeeze the Letters

### MATERIALS
Letters and Numbers reproducible (page 137)

resealable plastic bags

black felt

scissors

shampoo or tempera paint and liquid starch

Give each student a resealable plastic bag with a piece of black felt cut slightly smaller than the bag in it. Help each student partially fill his or her bag with shampoo or tempera paint mixed with liquid starch. Have students seal their bag tightly and place the sealed bag in a second bag as a backup in case the first one leaks. Give each student a copy of the Letters and Numbers reproducible. Invite students to use the reproducible as a guideline as they use their finger to draw on their bag the correct strokes for the letters and numbers. The felt will help make each letter or number appear for a few seconds before the student writes another one.

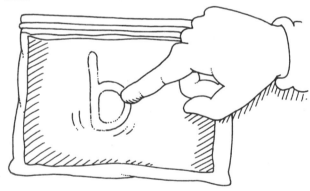

## Bump the Box

### MATERIALS
Bump the Box reproducible (page 138)

Have students use the Bump the Box reproducible to practice writing letters and numbers. Show students how to write each letter or number so it touches all sides of a square. Have students use the single squares for small letters and the double squares for tall and uppercase letters and letters that hang below the line. Filling an enclosed space gives students a sense of direction, builds their confidence, and helps them make uniform letters.

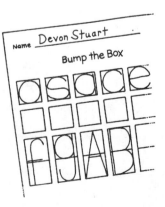

# Letters and Numbers

The Creative K-1 Classroom © 1999 Creative Teaching Press

Name _____    Date _____

# Bump the Box

# SHARED WRITING

Shared writing is modeled for the class and involves students. During shared writing, the teacher initiates and models writing, while students contribute ideas. Teacher and students work together to compose messages and stories. The teacher models how writing works and draws attention to letters, words, and sounds during the writing. The object of shared writing is to demonstrate and teach the necessary skills and conventions of fluent writing.

## Story Web

**MATERIALS**
chart paper
highlighters

Ask students to decide on a topic for a story, and record it on chart paper. Brainstorm with students a list of information and details for possible inclusion in a story. Ask students *What do you want people to know?* as a leading question. After information is recorded, review the chart. Ask *Which of these details belong together?* Highlight information that belongs together. For example, you could highlight physical traits in yellow, behaviors in blue, and information about the setting in pink. Determine with students the sequence of delivery, and write a finished story.

## Letter to a Character

**MATERIALS**

storybook
chart paper

Read a story to the class. Together, write a letter on chart paper to one of the characters in the story. Be certain to include at least one question. Send the letter to an upper-grade class, and ask them to respond as the character.

Dear Three Little Pigs,
We think you are very brave pigs. We are sorry that the wolf blew two of your houses down. Do you have enough money to rebuild the houses? Do you need our help?

## Story Starters

**MATERIALS**

Story Map (page 125)
old magazines
glue
paper stock
chart paper

Glue pictures from old magazines onto paper stock. Write words that relate to the pictures on the back of each paper for use with independent-writing activities. Display a picture. Ask students to think about it "in their minds." Continue to ask students questions which they answer only in their minds, such as *What is the main idea? What is happening in the picture? Who is in the picture? Where is it? When could this be happening?* and so on. After students have had thinking time, repeat the questions for group response, drawing a story map (see page 125) on chart paper to represent their comments. Use the story map to create a group story.

The Ice Cream That Never Melted
by Mrs. Paul's Class

One sunny day, a young girl found...

## Rewrites

**MATERIALS**

familiar story
chart paper

Read aloud a familiar story, such as *Rosie the Hen, The Lion and the Mouse,* or *Goldilocks and the Three Bears.* Use the story as the basis for creating a new story. Invite students to substitute the characters, setting, problem, or ending. Write the new story on chart paper.

# INTERACTIVE WRITING

Like shared writing, interactive writing involves the teacher and students working together to compose messages or stories. However, in interactive writing, the students also help record the words and interact with the process of recording the words.

During interactive writing, the teacher and students create text that is written word by word, with the teacher demonstrating the process and students participating in aspects of the writing. For example, students can help write familiar sight words in the text or the first letter of a word and the teacher completes it. Students may write a small word within a bigger word. Interactive writing provides students with letter-formation practice; opportunities to look for "word chunks," clusters, or patterns; experience with punctuation; and an increased awareness of differences between letters and words and spaces between words. Interactive writing does take time, but the benefits are worth it.

## Give Me a Hand at Writing

**MATERIALS**
chart paper
storybook

In advance, draw a large hand on chart paper. Before reading a story, ask students the title of the story, and record it on the palm of the hand. Invite volunteers to help you write some of the words in the title, such as *the* or *at*. Read the storybook to the class. Then, discuss with students the main idea of the story, and have them help you record it on the thumb. Discuss three events from the story, and with assistance from your students, write them on each of the next three fingers. Ask students about the ending of the story, and record it on the last finger.

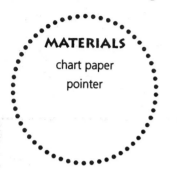

# Morning Message

**MATERIALS**

chart paper

pointer

The "Morning Message" is a perfect way to start a day. Engage students' interest each day with a Morning Message written on chart paper. Stimulate group input as you discuss the day's activities or reinforce concepts. Model the conventions of writing, including sentence structure and the use of descriptive words. As you write a Morning Message, think aloud as you write to the class, modeling capital letters, letter/sound relationship, letter formation, punctuation, and completeness of thought. Draw attention to rhyming words, sequence of events, and familiar words. You may even omit certain letters from words and encourage the students to discover what they are. Encourage students to find familiar words, circle punctuation marks and specific sounds, and add comments of their own. Read and reread the message as a group, having a volunteer point to each word. At the end of each week, bind the Morning Messages into a book to be kept in the Literacy Center or used as a Read the Room (see page 131) activity. Refer to the following list of elements to include in your Morning Message:

- date
- day's schedule
- attendance information
- theme information
- record of events
- explanation of events
- summary of events
- predictions
- opinions
- questions
- jokes ("funny ha-ha's")
- quotes
- lists
- vocabulary
- rhymes
- alliteration
- words missing vowels or consonants
- information about subjects studied

# Daily News

**MATERIALS**

Daily News reproducible
(page 143)

chart paper

bookbinding materials

Students enjoy voicing their contributions and watching as their words become print. Ask students *What did we do today?* at the end of each day. Write students' ideas sequentially on chart paper under the headings *Beginning, Middle,* and *End.* Students should also be encouraged to write words of their own on the chart as appropriate. Then, form a complete sentence, and write it on a copy of the Daily News reproducible. Students can copy the daily news on their own form and take it home at the end of the week. At the end of each month, bind the pages written together as a class into a book titled *Daily News,* and store it in your class library or Literacy Center for students to read.

# Daily News

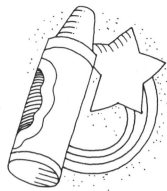

Week of _____

| Monday _____ |
| :--- |
| _____ |
| _____ |

| Tuesday _____ |
| :--- |
| _____ |
| _____ |

| Wednesday _____ |
| :--- |
| _____ |
| _____ |

| Thursday _____ |
| :--- |
| _____ |
| _____ |

| Friday _____ |
| :--- |
| _____ |
| _____ |

The Creative K–1 Classroom © 1999 Creative Teaching Press

# GUIDED WRITING

Guided writing is student initiated and teacher supported. Students engage in a variety of meaningful writing experiences, and the teacher provides instruction through mini-lessons and conferences. Guided writing is also referred to as Writer's Workshop. During guided writing, students construct their own writing with the teacher nearby for assistance, guidance, and feedback. Observe your students as they go through the writing process, and then conduct mini-lessons to address the specific needs of your students. Encourage students to increase the length of existing sentences by asking them relevant questions about their writing. For example, ask *What did it look like? What was it doing? Does it like to ____? Why?* As students progress in their writing, challenge them to make a four-word sentence or a six-word sentence.

## Literature Innovation

**MATERIALS**
familiar story
large sheets of construction paper
crayons or markers
bookbinding materials

Use a familiar story to create a new story. Follow the pattern of the first story, but have students change the setting, characters, problem, or solution. Record their story on large sheets of construction paper. Have students work in pairs to illustrate each page of the story. Bind the pages into a class big book, and store it in the class library or Literacy Center for students to reread.

## Splodges

**MATERIALS**

marker

poster board or
construction paper

Draw an unusual shape, or "splodge," on poster board or construction paper for each student. Have students trace around the picture and incorporate the shape into a new picture. Have students write or dictate a story about the shape below their picture.

## Shadow Writing

**MATERIALS**

writing paper
crayons or markers

For students who cannot write yet, invite them to dictate their own story. Record each student's words on penmanship lines, leaving a space between lines for the student to copy the words. Invite students to illustrate their story at the top of the page.

## Shadow Sentence

**MATERIALS**

writing paper
scissors
glue

Using the same process as Shadow Writing (above), invite each student to dictate one sentence, and record his or her words, leaving space for the student to copy your writing beneath. At the bottom of the page, write each of the dictated words out of sequence. Have students cut apart the words and glue them on the page in sequence.

## Descriptive Words

**MATERIALS**

paper
crayons or markers

Start with one thematic word and create a sentence frame for students to write an entire class book. Add a blank before the subject for students to add a descriptive word and leave a blank after the subject for students to complete the sentence with an action word. For example, write *The _____ bear _____, The _____ kite _____, The _____ snowman _____,* or *My _____ mother _____.* Copy the frame on paper for each student. Ask each student to complete and illustrate the sentence frame. Encourage students to extend their sentences by asking them *Where? Why?* or *How?* as appropriate.

## Fold a Story

**MATERIALS**

newsprint
crayons or colored pencils

Have each student fold a piece of newsprint into four sections and write one of the following words in each quadrant: *Beginning, Middle, Middle, End.* Ask students to illustrate a story in sequence from beginning to end. As students retell the story, record their words beneath each picture. Choose at least one word from each section for the child to write. Give guidance as needed.

## Mystery Object

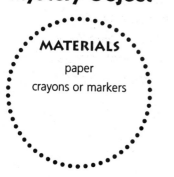
**MATERIALS**

paper
crayons or markers

Have each student describe an object in detail without identifying the object. Students can write what it is used for and by whom, where it might be found, and what it does. Prompt them to refer to the five senses where appropriate. Have students record the answer and an illustration on the back side of the page.

# INDEPENDENT WRITING

Independent writing is generated by students and requires little teacher support. Students write their own messages and stories, using known words and constructing spelling of unknown words. Students sometimes help each other, but mostly they refer to the print around them on word walls, on charts, in dictionaries, or on the computer. By observing students during independent writing, you can better plan for mini-lessons and writing tips to bring up during interactive writing.

## Post Office

**MATERIALS**
shoe box
gift wrap
scissors
letter-writing supplies

Create a permanent area in your classroom to represent a post office. Decorate a shoe box with gift wrap, and cut a slit in the top to drop in letters. Provide letter-writing supplies, such as a variety of paper and postcards, old greeting cards, envelopes, rubber stamps, ink pads, stickers, tracing templates, children's dictionaries, colored pens, pencils, crayons, scissors, glue, tape, receipt books, and name cards. Invite students to write letters to classmates, authors, family members, teachers, or members of the community.

## Pen Pals

### MATERIALS

class photos

scissors

class list

writing paper

envelopes

index cards

Duplicate class photos, and cut apart the photos to make "stamps." Keep one set of the stamps in your post office at a time. Invite students to write as many letters as they want, but only to a student whose picture appears on one of the stamps. This will ensure that each student will receive a letter before the cycle begins again. Keep a class list in the post office so that the students can refer to it when writing their letters and addressing the envelopes. Write some letter-writing phrases on index cards, and store them at the post office to provide students with story starters, ideas, or prompts to write about if they run out of ideas.

## Talk It Through

### MATERIALS

stuffed animals

puppets

paper

Never underestimate the influence of props in creative story writing. Invite students to interact with stuffed animals and puppets. Stories will often naturally emerge from their interaction with the props. Invite each student to perform a story for the class. After each performance, ask students to identify the beginning, middle, and end of their story. Then, invite them to write the story they performed.

## Grab Bag

### MATERIALS

index cards

bag

paper

crayons or markers

Write sight words on index cards, and place them in a bag. Have partners each take a card out of the bag. Have partners work together to make up one sentence using the two words they drew. Invite each student to write or dictate the sentence and illustrate it.

# CREATING AND MANAGING CENTERS

Meeting the individual needs of 20–30 students every day can be a demanding responsibility. Teach to their diverse needs by using a variety of instructional methods. Learning centers are highly useful tools for accomplishing this goal. Learning centers as described in this book are places with an organized set of activities in which students independently (or with minimal supervision) learn, practice, and apply skills introduced in small-group or whole-group instruction. Whether you choose to introduce or model a concept, or allow for practice and application, the center is designed to support and nurture students in an intimate setting. By limiting the number of students for direct instruction, you can more closely monitor attention and skill acquisition. This increases the effectiveness of activities and fosters more freedom for individual differences in learning.

This section begins with frequently asked questions about centers and then provides ideas for four common centers: ABC, Literacy, Math, and Think and Do. Use these centers to integrate the ever-increasing amount of curriculum you need to cover.

The use of learning centers will

♥ help you attend to students' diverse needs.

♥ ease the implementation of an ever-growing curriculum.

♥ provide opportunities to individualize instruction.

♥ facilitate students' ability to make choices and gain social skills.

♥ increase all students' participation in hands-on learning.

♥ increase the integration of curriculum areas.

♥ provide each student with the benefits of small-group instruction, individual exploration, and cooperative learning.

## How Many Centers Should I Use?

Having four learning centers is manageable for most classrooms and allows for a broad range of activities within each. You can customize your centers to make the best use of your space, materials, and needs. Ideas are included for four common centers on pages 153–156. You can adapt a great deal of your curriculum to work within these centers. Center suggestions are also included in the Terrific Topics section (pages 161–217).

## What Are Learning Centers?

Learning centers as described in this book are places with an organized set of activities in which students independently (or with minimal supervision) practice and enhance skills introduced during small-group or whole-group instruction.

## How Many Activities Should Be at Each Center?

Two or three activity choices at each center are sufficient. Providing students with a choice helps them make decisions and gives them a sense of empowerment. Too many choices, however, result in a mess to clean up and some students never venturing beyond the same activity. Permit students to use only the materials you put out, and rotate these materials regularly. By not having access to the same activities over and over, interest is kept high and students are exposed to a variety of activities and skills.

## Where Do Centers Go?

Permanent arrangements of furniture and materials are not always an option. If possible, have a table for each center and materials for the activities stored nearby. But, where space is limited, other options are equally suitable. A four-drawer cardboard dresser, for example, can easily hold the materials for each center. One drawer for each center makes setup and cleanup a snap. Learning center materials can also be stored in clear plastic boxes with lids. These make the contents easy to identify and are convenient for stacking on shelves.

## Who Goes Where?

Use the Learning Center Wheel (page 159) to divide the class into separate mixed-ability work groups. Copy the Learning Center Wheel on tagboard. Cut out a 3" (7.5 cm) circle from tagboard, divide it into four equal sections, and color each section a different color. Use a brass fastener to attach the colored circle to the center of the Learning Center Wheel to create a spinner. Divide the class into four working groups. Assign each group a color. Turn the circle when you want groups to move to a different center. Have the class refer to the Learning Center Wheel to determine which center they go to. Students will know which center to work at based on the position of the color circle on the learning center chart.

## How Do I Transition the Groups from One Center to the Next?

When the time is up at the center, have students clean their center and prepare it for the next group. Gather students together to highlight successes and evaluate behavior. Give further instruction or explain special needs before dismissing them to their next center.

## Should I Reserve Centers for Free-Choice Time?

Centers can be used for free-choice time, but for all students to benefit from the provided activities, use learning centers as an integral part of the curriculum for 50–60 minutes a day for as many days each week as you desire.

## How Can I Explicitly Instruct Students at the Centers?

Explicit instruction can occur prior to center time as whole-group instruction, in small groups at the centers, or individually at the centers. Clearly describe the process for each center. You can post it on the board or at each center, or watch for a few minutes until students are working independently. When you observe a student who needs assistance, give him or her a direct lesson while the other students are working independently. If all students at the center have the same problem, give a mini-lesson for the group.

## How Long Should Students Spend at the Centers?

Use the centers for two 25–30 minute periods each day. This consistent time period teaches students to work within a time frame, keeps attention high, and limits behavior problems because of the movement it allows. Work does not need to be finished in one day; it may be carried over. This time allows you an opportunity to teach one-on-one and in small groups.

## How Do I Assess Learning at the Centers?

Attach a copy of the Workshop Contract (page 160) to the cover of each student's folder. Prepare each contract one week at a time. Individualize the contracts to address specific needs, or make class contracts with multiple activity choices. After each task is completed, you or a volunteer circles completed work and marks a plus for superior work, a check for adequate work, or a minus for work that needs improvement. There is room for volunteers to jot down a note, such as *Repeat another time, Done with help, Too hard—re-teach,* or *Too easy.* There is also a place to make a daily record of each student's behavior and effective use of time. These daily records help you adjust your teaching, individualize your instruction, and stay current with each student's ability and growth.

## How Do Students Work at the Centers?

Students can work independently, with partners, or in small groups at the centers. Working with a partner helps ensure that students meet their goals with one checking up on the other. Students of mixed abilities work well side by side, teaching or learning from the other, or working independently at their own level.

## Can I Manage Centers with No Outside Help?

You do not have to have volunteers or aides to effectively use centers. Work at one center while students are working on uncomplicated activities. Train your students to govern themselves and seek assistance from their group members at the beginning of the year. Begin with very simple tasks and short periods of time. For example, in the ABC Center have students do alphabet dot-to-dots or match alphabet macaroni to lowercase letters; in the Math Center have students play War with playing cards or use linking cubes or pattern blocks to make patterns; in the Literacy Center have students use flannel-board pieces or puppets to retell stories; in the Think and Do Center have students experiment with magnets or draw pictures. As students demonstrate their understanding of your rules, goals, and expectations, increase the time given and the difficulty of the tasks.

## Do I Need Parent Volunteers?

Parent volunteers can enhance the effectiveness of learning centers, but are not required to make the program successful. If you have a partner or aide who works with you during the day, use his or her assistance to supervise one of the centers. If there are only two adults to work at the centers, use them to supervise the ABC Center and the Math Center. Activities can be planned for the Literacy Center and Think and Do Center that require the students to work independently (or with minimal supervision). If you have no helpers, supervise the ABC or Math center, and have independent-practice activities in the other centers. In this situation, centers would probably be most efficient if limited to 20-minute periods of time.

## How Can I Use Volunteers at My Centers?

Solicit the help of parent volunteers in your classroom. Give volunteers worthwhile tasks, and challenge them to commit to working regularly in your classroom. Train your volunteers so they are informed on what to do and how to do it. With the assistance of parent volunteers, learning centers function for the purpose of individualizing the curriculum to the needs of each student. It is ideal to have one committed parent at each of the four centers. (See Parent Training on page 33 for advice on how to train your volunteers.) Where volunteers are used as teachers for each center, offer a lesson of skills instruction in each center with time for practice and application. Also, with trained volunteers at the centers, you are free to call students to your desk and individualize their learning. This way you can assess your students daily while the class works at the centers.

# ABC CENTER

The ABC Center provides students with an opportunity to practice working with letters and the alphabetic principle. Students identify and match letters and letter sounds, manipulate letters to make words, and practice writing letters.

See the following lists for activity and material suggestions for the ABC Center. Look for the ABC icon in the Terrific Topics section to find additional ABC Center activities.

## ACTIVITIES

- ♥ making words
- ♥ practicing spelling
- ♥ sequencing letters in alphabetical order
- ♥ practicing penmanship
- ♥ reviewing dictionary skills
- ♥ matching uppercase and lowercase letters
- ♥ participating in phonemic awareness activities
- ♥ doing letter-recognition activities

## MATERIALS

- ♥ word cards and matching objects
- ♥ computers
- ♥ alphabet games
- ♥ vowel and consonant flash cards
- ♥ rhyming picture cards and objects
- ♥ letter tiles
- ♥ writing paper
- ♥ poems, songs, and chants
- ♥ alphabet strips
- ♥ sight word flash cards
- ♥ pocket chart
- ♥ picture dictionaries
- ♥ magnetic letters

# LITERACY CENTER

The Literacy Center provides students with an opportunity to develop reading and pre-reading skills, understand concepts of print, and explore story writing and storytelling.

See the following lists for activity and material suggestions for the Literacy Center. Look for the book icon in the Terrific Topics section to find additional Literacy Center activities.

## ACTIVITIES
- ♥ sequencing stories
- ♥ playing with puppets
- ♥ using flannel boards
- ♥ writing in journals
- ♥ doing creative writing
- ♥ listening
- ♥ acting in reader's theater
- ♥ reading a variety of books
- ♥ reading the room
- ♥ storytelling

## MATERIALS
- ♥ listening post
- ♥ flannel board
- ♥ puppets
- ♥ magnetic stories
- ♥ journals
- ♥ class post office
- ♥ book nook (class library)
- ♥ class books and rewrites
- ♥ poems, songs, and rhymes
- ♥ pocket chart
- ♥ props for dramatizing stories

# 123

# MATH CENTER

The Math Center provides students with an opportunity to practice different mathematical concepts, such as problem solving, estimating, graphing, patterning, sorting, and measuring. See the following lists for activity and material suggestions for the Math Center. Look for the 123 icon in the Terrific Topics section to find additional Math Center activities.

## ACTIVITIES
- ♥ measuring
- ♥ graphing
- ♥ problem solving
- ♥ estimating
- ♥ practicing number facts
- ♥ patterning
- ♥ sorting
- ♥ counting
- ♥ doing number-recognition activities
- ♥ sequencing numbers
- ♥ writing numerals
- ♥ counting by evens and odds
- ♥ counting by fives and tens

## MATERIALS
- ♥ pattern blocks
- ♥ objects for sorting
- ♥ money
- ♥ objects for comparing
- ♥ numbers to sequence
- ♥ Peg-Boards
- ♥ base ten blocks
- ♥ dice
- ♥ playing cards
- ♥ number games
- ♥ linking cubes
- ♥ Venn diagrams
- ♥ measuring materials
- ♥ computers
- ♥ clocks
- ♥ counters
- ♥ graphs

# THINK AND DO CENTER

The Think and Do Center provides students with the opportunity to think, explore, and create. Students problem solve, create art projects, and investigate objects and concepts on a deeper level. See the following lists for activity and material suggestions for the Think and Do Center. Look for the lightbulb icon in the Terrific Topics section to find additional Think and Do Center activities.

## ACTIVITIES

- ♥ creating theme-related art projects
- ♥ experimenting with and exploring science concepts
- ♥ doing puzzles
- ♥ playing dominoes
- ♥ working with computers
- ♥ investigating objects
- ♥ sorting and classifying
- ♥ sculpting, drawing, and painting

## MATERIALS

- ♥ puzzles
- ♥ checkers
- ♥ easel art
- ♥ play dough
- ♥ pentominoes
- ♥ tangrams
- ♥ science materials
- ♥ pattern blocks
- ♥ attribute blocks
- ♥ beads
- ♥ Legos®
- ♥ computers
- ♥ objects to sort and classify
- ♥ microscope
- ♥ magnets

# DISCOVERY TIME

Discovery Time is a variation on learning centers in which students have free-choice time at learning centers or other pre-determined activities, such as playing with blocks, playing house, making art, or using manipulatives. There is no accountability, no reporting, no task for students to complete; it is a time for students to explore and discover. For the most part, Discovery Time is child-centered without adult intervention, whereas learning centers use adult volunteers as much as possible for direct instruction. Give students the same two or three choices you would during learning center time, but without guidelines to complete a task. You may want to set out the materials for the following week's guided instruction so students will have an opportunity to explore them beforehand. The following page provides answers to common questions about Discovery Time. See the lists below for activity and material suggestions for Discovery Time.

## ACTIVITIES

- ♥ participating in sand play
- ♥ participating in water play
- ♥ listening to books on tape
- ♥ participating in dramatic play
- ♥ graphing
- ♥ sorting
- ♥ painting
- ♥ drawing
- ♥ exploring science concepts
- ♥ reading the room
- ♥ doing phonemic awareness activities
- ♥ doing alphabet awareness activities

## MATERIALS

- ♥ blocks
- ♥ Legos®
- ♥ puzzles
- ♥ puppets
- ♥ magnets
- ♥ magnifying glass
- ♥ objects to classify and sort
- ♥ flannel-board stories
- ♥ class-made books
- ♥ storybooks
- ♥ playhouse
- ♥ exploration table
- ♥ writing materials
- ♥ pattern blocks
- ♥ attribute blocks
- ♥ dress-up clothes
- ♥ beads
- ♥ computers
- ♥ microscope

## How Often Do I Use Discovery Time?

For kindergarten students, have each group go to two learning centers four days a week and Discovery Time every day. Plan for first graders to go to two learning centers four days a week and Discovery Time one day a week. Discovery Time in first grade involves the self-selection of predetermined learning center activities that you set out to introduce or reinforce specific concepts. In first grade, students do not get blocks, dress-up clothes, or a playhouse. Instead, they get mild "brain strain" activities that involve problem solving, thinking, and writing, such as working with do-it-yourself math manipulatives, compound words, or suffix and prefix manipulatives. The students explore these activities during an allotted period of time, and you are freed to work with individuals or small groups as needed.

## Why Have Discovery Time?

Capitalizing on a child's curiosity and innate inclination to play is the primary focus of Discovery Time. It invites students to make their own choices by providing a variety of playful learning experiences designed to enhance specific units of study or themes. Students need the opportunity to explore and discover on their own to develop oral language, social interaction, creative thinking, fine-motor coordination, and problem-solving skills.

## How Can I Use Discovery Time to Assess Students?

Use Discovery Time to call individual students to your desk for Prescriptive Teaching (see page 58) and individualized assessment. Prescriptive Teaching and assessment happen one-on-one each day during Discovery Time and also during learning center time if there is a sufficient number of adults in the room to run the centers. Also, use this time to simply observe students and their thought processes. This is a valuable time for you to meet student needs at an individual level.

# Learning Center Wheel

Name _____

Week of _____

# Workshop Contract

| Center | Monday | Tuesday | Wednesday | Thursday | Friday |
|--------|--------|---------|-----------|----------|--------|
| ABC |  |  |  |  |  |
|  📖 |  |  |  |  |  |
| 123 |  |  |  |  |  |
|  💡 |  |  |  |  |  |
| Effective use of time: | − ✓ + | − ✓ + | − ✓ + | − ✓ + | − ✓ + |
| Quality of work: | − ✓ + | − ✓ + | − ✓ + | − ✓ + | − ✓ + |

The Creative K–1 Classroom © 1999 Creative Teaching Press

# TERRIFIC TOPICS

The activities in this section are designed to complement common themes taught throughout the year. They are organized by months of the year, but be sure to integrate the ideas at whatever point they best extend your curriculum. The thematic ideas include whole-group, small-group, and learning center activities. Activities that can work at one of the four centers described on pages 153–156 are indicated by the icons below.

Begin each theme by inviting students to brainstorm a list of words that are related to the theme, and write them on index cards, thematic cutouts, or chart paper for use in learning center work. Then, enlarge the suggested poem or song on chart paper or display it on sentence strips in a pocket chart. Read it aloud, pointing to (or sliding a pointer under) each word. Give a copy of the poem or song to each student. Invite students to draw illustrations next to the text. Bind related poems and songs with a construction-paper cover into individual books. As you read from the enlarged copy of each poem or song at the front of the room, have students follow along in their own book, pointing to each word to reinforce print and phonemic awareness skills. Have students use a colored pencil to highlight rhyming words, sounds you are emphasizing, or certain onsets or rimes that reappear throughout the text. Have students look for familiar words, rhyming words, spaces between words, capital letters, and punctuation on the charts and sentence strips. Count the number of words in a sentence, and show students that a sentence does not necessarily end at the end of a line. Change the meaning of the poem or song by placing sticky notes with new words over the original words.

ABC . . . **ABC Center**

📖 . . . **Literacy Center**

123 . . . **Math Center**

💡 . . . **Think and Do Center**

# Me and My Friends

## I've Got a Friend

*(sing to the tune of "Bingo")*

I've got a friend named _____.

Can you clap his (her) name?

*(Clap syllables while saying the child's name.)*

Listen closely, you will hear

One name stands out loud and clear.

Do you know whose name you hear?

Can you guess his (her) name?

*(Clap the syllables in the name.)*

## We Are Friends

 Discuss with students how true friends want what is best for each other and do not tell each other to do things they should not. Teach the song "True Friendship" to your students. Invite students to draw themselves with a friend. Copy the song onto a sheet of construction paper for each student. Have students cut out their picture and glue it to the paper.

🎵 **True Friendship**
*(sing to the tune of "A-Tisket, A-Tasket")*

A friend will never ask me
To do what I should not.
I won't get mad if I get teased.
True friendship can't be bought.

## We Are Alike; We Are Different

Write on separate index cards different things kids can do (e.g., *ride a bike, skip, sing, speak another language*). Use chalk to draw two interlocking circles on the chalkboard or put tape on an old plastic tablecloth to create a Venn diagram. Select two students, ask each to choose a circle, and label the circles with each student's name. Invite students to read each card and place it in the part of the circles that best describes which person can do what. Repeat the activity with different students. To extend learning, encourage students to add their own ideas to the list.

## Toss and Tumble

**ABC** Write the letters of a student's name on separate index cards. Shuffle the cards, and toss them on the floor. Select students to take a card and arrange themselves in sequence to spell the student's name. If the game is played as a mystery, knowing that the capital letter comes first will be helpful in identifying whose name it is. As the "mystery" student recognizes his or her own name, he or she may help arrange the students in proper sequence.

## I Can Do Anything

Copy the song below on chart paper or on sentence strips and place them in a pocket chart. Teach the song to the class. Invite students to create actions to go with the song.

**I Can Do Anything**
*(sing to the tune of "Three Blind Mice")*

I can do anything.
I can do anything.
If I try.
If I try.
I've got all the power.
I've got all the strength
To do and be what I want
If I just try.

## Name Sort

**ABC** Write the first name of each student on a separate index card. Glue or tape student photos to the name cards to aid in name recognition. Invite students to choose two or three cards at a time and place them in alphabetical order. Older students can write each set of names in order.

## The Best Thing about Me

Read aloud *The Important Book.* Have students use the language pattern from the book to write about themselves. Challenge each student to complete the sentence frames below on separate sheets of construction paper, incorporating things about themselves. Invite students to illustrate each page. Bind each student's pages together to make a book titled *The Best Things about Me!* Invite students to share their book with classmates or family members. For additional learning, invite students to make an important book for a friend or family member.

*The best thing about _____ is he/she is _____.*
*He/she _____.*
*He/she _____.*
*He/she _____.*
*But the best thing about _____ is he/she is _____.*

## Marvelous Me

**MATERIALS**

Marvelous Me reproducible
(page 167)

crayons or markers

scissors

construction paper

glue

class photos

bookbinding materials

canvas bag

Give each student a copy of the Marvelous Me reproducible. Invite students to write or dictate a response for each sentence frame. Have students cut out the sentence frames and glue them to separate sheets of construction paper. Ask students to illustrate each sentence frame. Glue each student's photo to a piece of construction paper to make a book cover. Have students trace their handprints on each side of their photograph. Bind each student's pages together to make a book titled *Marvelous Me.* Place the books in a canvas bag. Each weekend, send the bag home with a different student. Invite students to read a book from the bag to learn about a classmate. Ask students to share with the class what they learned about their classmate. Have students return the bag so others can have a chance to take home the bag.

## Name Cheer

**MATERIALS**

magnetic letters

Have students spotlight their classmates and create rhymes with the cheer below. Challenge students to think of a word that rhymes with the student's name and incorporate the name and the rhyming word into a sentence to end the cheer. For example, *Bill, Bill, climb the hill* could be the ending to the cheer below. Model and teach how letters have to be in a particular order to spell a word. Use magnetic letters to spell the name, and then point to each letter. Then, try spelling the name backwards. Discuss how this does not say the person's name. Rearrange the magnetic letters to illustrate this as you sing. Have the class cheer the student's name when they see the letters in the correct order.

Give me a B
*B*
Give me an I
*I*
Give me an L
*L*
Give me another L
*L*
What have we got?
*Bill*
What did you say?
*Bill*

# Marvelous Me

My name is _____.

I am _____ years old.

My birthday is _____.

My favorite color is _____.

I am good at _____.

My favorite sport is _____.

My favorite story is _____.

My favorite song is _____.

I like to _____ and _____ in my free time.

Here is a picture of my family.

I love my family because _____.

Here is a picture of my pet.

I am happy when _____.

I am good at _____.

My favorite food is _____.

I don't like _____.

If I were an animal I would be _____.

When I am 30 years old, I _____.

# Pumpkins and Leaves

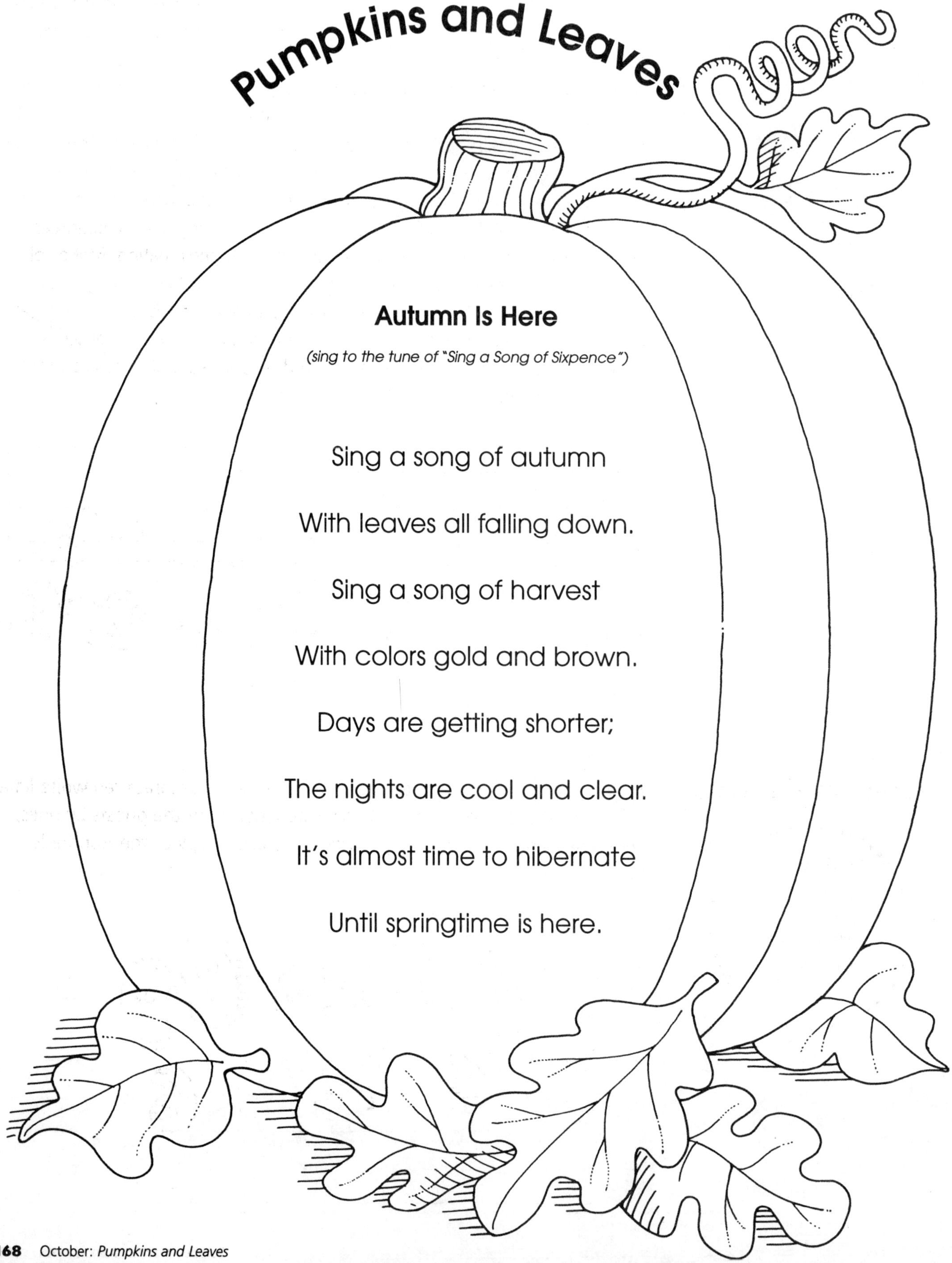

## Autumn Is Here

*(sing to the tune of "Sing a Song of Sixpence")*

Sing a song of autumn

With leaves all falling down.

Sing a song of harvest

With colors gold and brown.

Days are getting shorter;

The nights are cool and clear.

It's almost time to hibernate

Until springtime is here.

## Edit and Eat

**ABC** Write on sentence strips simple seasonal sentences that have capitalization and/or punctuation mistakes, such as *lets carve a pumpkin said mark, its windy, this is my rake,* and *can i have some apple pie.* Invite students to use small food items to make all corrections on the sentence strips. Bugles snacks make cute exclamation points. Straight pretzels make exclamation points and straight letters. Peanuts work well for commas and quotation marks. Alphabet cereal can be used for capital letters. Cheerios or Kix cereal works for periods. Pretzel twists with a few bites out of them make question marks. Browse the cracker section of the market to find exciting foods that can be used for other punctuation. After you or a volunteer checks the sentences for accuracy, the students can begin eating. Make colored sets of sentence strips, numbering them on the back according to the difficulty of the task. For example, include short vowel words and missing capital letters in set #1, long vowel words and missing end marks in set #2, a combination of both in set #3, a list of words in a series that needs commas in set #4, and missing quotation marks in set # 5.

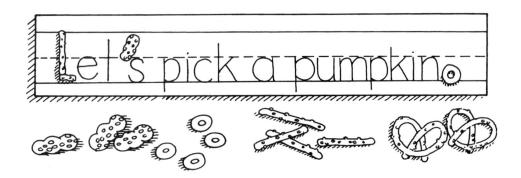

## Lima Bean Ghosts

**123** Invite each student to use a black marker to decorate ten white lima beans to make "ghosts." Have students count the ghosts by ones, twos, fives, and tens. Encourage students to use a copy of the Hundreds Chart for help.

## Pumpkin ABC

**MATERIALS**

Pumpkins reproducible
(page 172)

scissors

glue

paper

**ABC** Write a letter on each pumpkin on the Pumpkins reproducible. Give a copy of the revised reproducible to each student, and have students cut out each pumpkin. Ask students to alphabetize the letters and glue them in order on a sheet of paper.

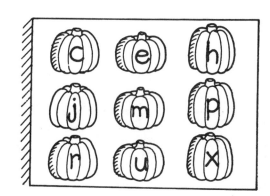

## Pumpkin Pitch

**MATERIALS**

empty plastic pumpkin

butcher paper

masking tape

candy corn

Place an empty plastic pumpkin on the floor in the middle of a large piece of butcher paper. Use masking tape to make a line on the floor about 5' (1.5 m) in front of the pumpkin. Challenge students to take turns standing behind the line and tossing candy corn into the pumpkin. Allow students to eat the candy in the pumpkin after everyone has had a turn.

## Pumpkin Bowling

**MATERIALS**

empty milk cartons

masking tape

pumpkin

Arrange empty milk cartons like bowling pins. Use masking tape to make a line on the floor about 5' (1.5 m) away from the cartons. Have students take turns standing behind the line and trying to knock over as many "pins" as possible by rolling a pumpkin toward the milk cartons.

# Hundreds Chart

| 1 | 2 | 3 | 4 | 5 | 6 | 7 | 8 | 9 | 10 |
|---|---|---|---|---|---|---|---|---|---|
| 11 | 12 | 13 | 14 | 15 | 16 | 17 | 18 | 19 | 20 |
| 21 | 22 | 23 | 24 | 25 | 26 | 27 | 28 | 29 | 30 |
| 31 | 32 | 33 | 34 | 35 | 36 | 37 | 38 | 39 | 40 |
| 41 | 42 | 43 | 44 | 45 | 46 | 47 | 48 | 49 | 50 |
| 51 | 52 | 53 | 54 | 55 | 56 | 57 | 58 | 59 | 60 |
| 61 | 62 | 63 | 64 | 65 | 66 | 67 | 68 | 69 | 70 |
| 71 | 72 | 73 | 74 | 75 | 76 | 77 | 78 | 79 | 80 |
| 81 | 82 | 83 | 84 | 85 | 86 | 87 | 88 | 89 | 90 |
| 91 | 92 | 93 | 94 | 95 | 96 | 97 | 98 | 99 | 100 |

# Pumpkins

# Thanksgiving and Gratitude

## I Am So Very Thankful

*(sing to the tune of "Do Your Ears Hang Low?")*

I am so very thankful

For many different things.

I have my friends and family

And all the love they bring.

I eat meals three times a day

And still have time for play.

I am so very thankful for many different things.

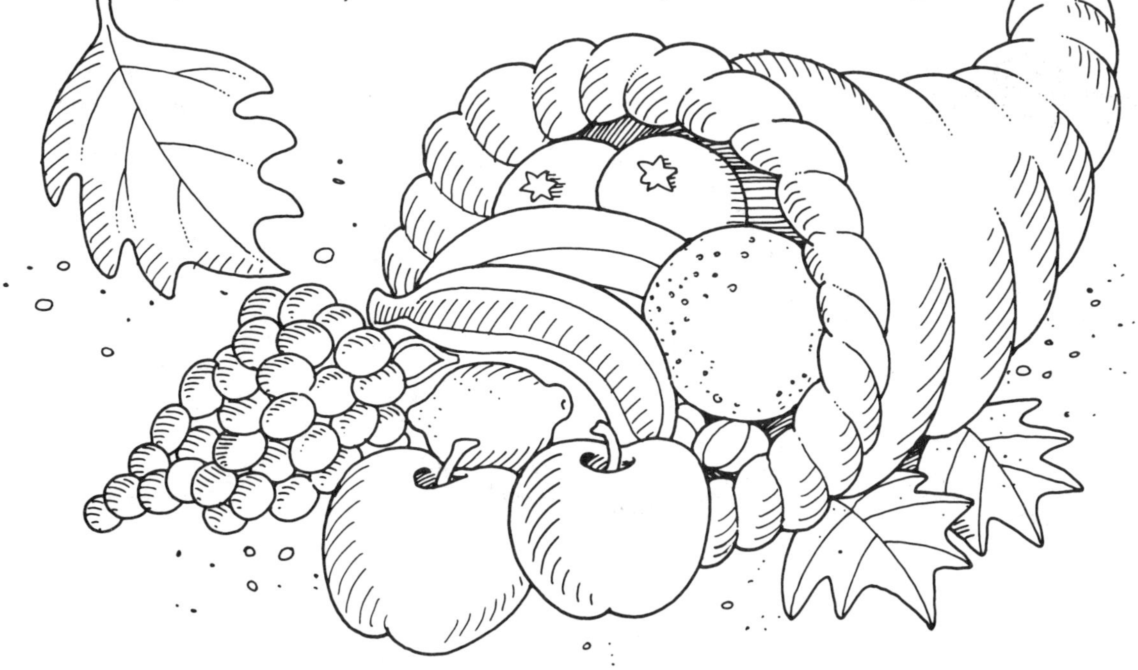

## Our Dictionary of Thankfulness

**MATERIALS**

hole punch

paper

three-ring binder

crayons or colored pencils

**ABC** Invite students to contribute an idea to a dictionary of things for which they are thankful. Hole-punch 26 pieces of paper, and place them in a three-ring binder titled *Our Dictionary of Thankfulness*. Write a letter of the alphabet on each page. Invite each student to select a letter page to illustrate. Tell students to write the name of something or someone for which or whom they are thankful that starts with the letter on their page. Encourage students to illustrate their work and place their page back into the binder.

## Turkey Feathers

**MATERIALS**

Feathers reproducible (page 177)

scissors

large and small cardboard circles

construction paper (assorted colors)

glue

crayons or markers

**123** Make two copies of the Feathers reproducible for each student. Ask students to write a numeral from 1–10 on each feather and cut out the feathers. Give each student one large and one small cardboard circle. Tell students to trace each circle on a piece of brown construction paper and cut out the circles. Have students glue the small circle onto the large circle to create a head for a turkey. Ask students to glue the large circle that forms the turkey's body onto a different-colored sheet of construction paper. Invite students to arrange their feathers in numerical order behind the larger circle to create a tail and then glue them in place. Encourage students to use construction-paper scraps and crayons or markers to add facial features and legs to their turkey.

## Our Thankful Class

**MATERIALS**

paper
camera/film or crayons

Invite students to write or dictate a letter to their parents. Have students tell why they are thankful for their parents. Start them off with the sentence frame *I'm thankful for you because _____*. Take a photograph of each student and place it on his or her letter, or have students draw a self-portrait.

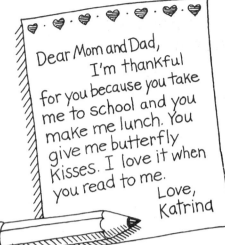

Dear Mom and Dad,
I'm thankful for you because you take me to school and you make me lunch. You give me butterfly kisses. I love it when you read to me.
Love,
Katrina

## Blanket Weaving

**MATERIALS**

6" x 8" (15 cm x 20 cm) cardboard pieces
scissors
string
brightly colored yarn

For each student, cut five or seven notches in each side of a 6" x 8" piece of cardboard. Invite students to wrap a piece of string from the first notch on one end down to the first notch on the other end. Then, have them wrap the string behind the notch and take it back to the top of the cardboard, wrapping it behind the second notch and back down to the bottom of the cardboard. Have students continue this until all notches have been wrapped. Show students how to tie the string off diagonally on the back side of the cardboard. Cut brightly colored yarn into 8" (20 cm) pieces. Have students weave the yarn through their loom, over and under the string, leaving fringe on each side. Have students continue to weave until the "blanket" is complete.

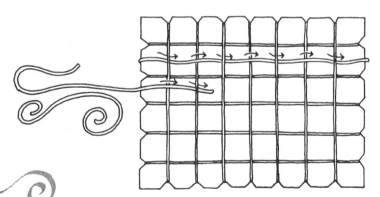

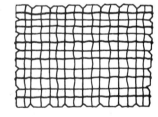

## Corny Gift of Thanks

**MATERIALS**

"Corny" poem
candy corn
resealable plastic bags

Place candy corn and a copy of the poem below in resealable plastic bags as thank-you gifts for parent volunteers.

**Corny**
This may be "corny,"
But we think you're great.
'Cause everything you do
Is always first-rate!

## Legends by the Campfire

**MATERIALS**

white twinkle lights

2' (61 cm) cardboard square

red and orange cellophane

small branches

extension cord

Attach white twinkle lights to a 2' square piece of cardboard, and cover it with red and orange cellophane and a few small branches to make a "campfire." Be sure to leave enough of the electric cord out of the fire to plug in to an extension cord. Turn out the lights, plug in the campfire, and invite students to retell their favorite Native American legend or the coming of the pilgrims to America. Invite students to drum the floor with their palms for sound effects to open the storytelling time.

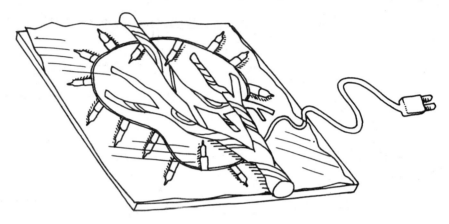

## Thank-You Sign

**MATERIALS**

"Thank You" song

construction paper

crayons or markers

scissors

glue or tape

Talk with students about how sometimes we receive one thing but may have wanted a different one. For example, sometimes we want a different color of paper or flavor of ice cream. Tell them how students with manners do not whine or beg; they accept what they get and they say *Thank you,* or they get nothing at all. Teach students the song "Thank You." Then, explain that saying *thank you* in sign language is similar to blowing a kiss (as shown). Copy the song onto a sheet of construction paper for each student. Invite each student to draw a self-portrait on the paper. Then, have students cut out an arm shape from another sheet of construction paper. Demonstrate to students how to glue or tape the arm to their paper so that the hand moves from the mouth out to show the sign for *thank you.*

Cassie

 **Thank You**
*(sing to the tune of "The Wheels on the Bus")*

You get what you get, and you say "Thank you."
You say "Thank you." You say "Thank you."
You get what you get, and you say "Thank you."
Thank you very much!
You're welcome!

# Feathers

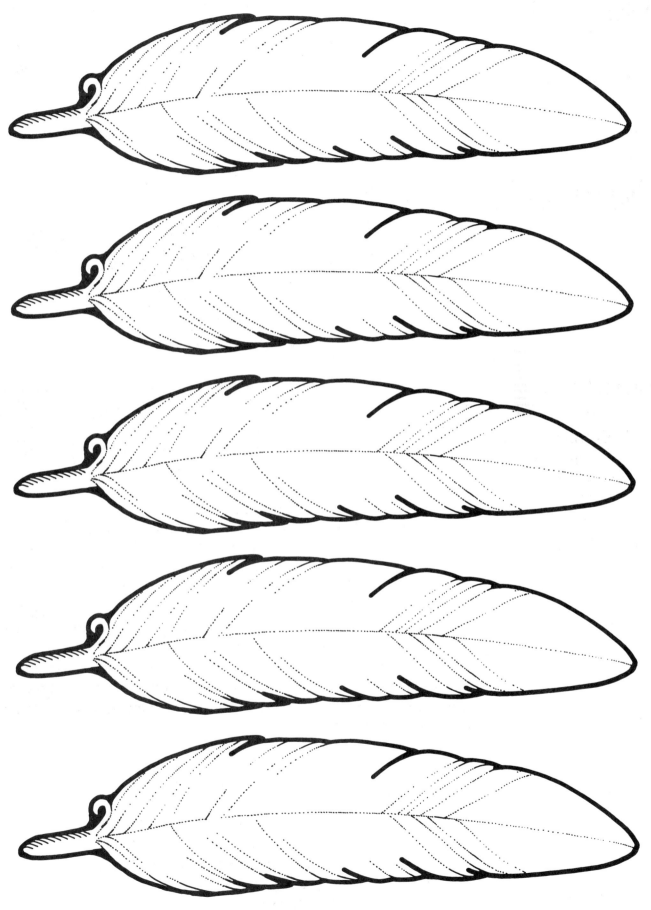

# Winter

## What Happens to a Snowflake?

What happens to a snowflake

*(Stand and shrug shoulders.)*

When it falls out of the sky?

*(Fall to the ground in a ball.)*

Does it fall into pieces?
Does it melt?

*(Spread arms out.)*

Does it cry?

*(Wipe eyes.)*

Or does it laugh and wiggle

*(Hold belly and wiggle.)*

As it plays in the snow?
I'm not a snowflake,

*(Point to self.)*

So I guess I'll never know.

*(Shrug shoulders.)*

## Ice Cubes

**MATERIALS**

Rhyming Words Picture
Cards (pages 113–115)

half-pint milk cartons

scissors

clear packing
tape

**ABC** Make a cube by cutting off the tops of two half-pint milk cartons and inserting the top of one into the top of another. Use clear packing tape to attach a picture from the Rhyming Words Picture Cards to each side of the cube. Tell students that the cube they are rolling is an "ice cube." Invite students to roll the cube and name a word that rhymes with the picture shown. Make several cubes with different pictures of objects that make easy rhymes. Store the cubes at the ABC Center for individual practice.

## Picture Talk

**MATERIALS**

*The Snowman* by
Raymond Briggs

paper

removable tape or
sticky notes

Invite each student to "read" the wordless picture book *The Snowman* to a partner. Create text for each story by writing the student's story on paper and using removable tape to attach it to the book. You can also write the student's story on sticky notes and place them in the book.

The boy and the snowman flew high into the air.

## Numbered Snowmen

**123** In advance, cut out eleven white 2" (5 cm) construction-paper "snowballs" for each student. Have students number their snowballs from 0–100, by tens. Ask students to glue their snowballs to a sheet of 4" x 24" (10 cm x 61 cm) construction paper to make a snowman with 0 on the bottom and 100 at the top. Have students cut out a hat and arms from construction paper and glue them to their numbered snowman. Invite students to use the zeros in 100 to make snowman eyes on the face. Have students point to the snowballs on their snowman while counting by tens for skip-counting practice.

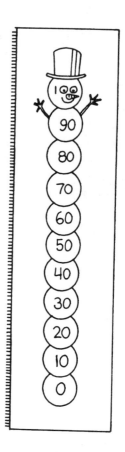

## Stick-It-to-Me

In advance, prepare this game by writing one-syllable, winter-related words (e.g., *coat, glove, hat, cap, cold, ice, snow, wet, boot, sled*) on craft sticks, one word per stick, writing it on both sides of one end of the stick. On five additional sticks, make a red dot on both sides. On another five sticks, make a green dot on both sides. Place the sticks in a juice can, word and dot side down. The first player draws a stick and follows these directions:

- If a word is drawn, it must be read correctly in order to keep the stick. Play then passes to the next player.
- If a red dot is drawn, the player loses his or her turn and returns the stick to the can.
- If a green dot is drawn, the player keeps it and then draws again.

Play continues until all word sticks have been removed from the can.

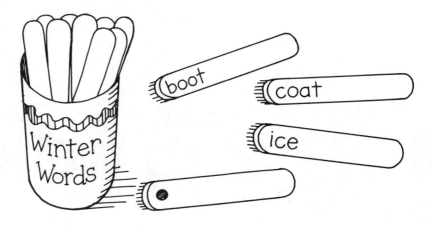

## Fittin' on a Mitten

**123** Read *The Mitten* to students. Encourage students to discuss the way that so many animals found shelter in the mitten. Give each student a copy of the Mittens reproducible to color. Ask students to predict how many objects (e.g., pennies) will cover each mitten. Invite students to then find the actual number. Have students repeat the process with other small objects, such as linking cubes.

16 pennies

## Matching Mittens

Copy the Mittens reproducible on different colors of paper, and cut out the mittens. Invite students to arrange the mittens into different categories and then make a pattern. Or, write pairs of rhyming words, homophones, or opposite words on the cutouts, and encourage students to match the mittens in each pair.

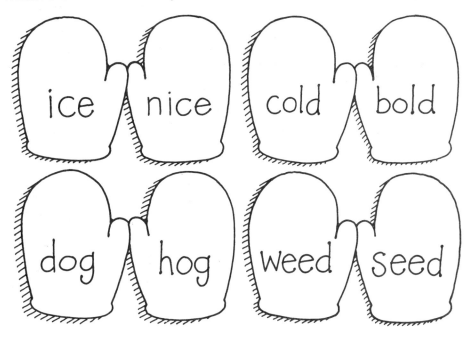

# Mittens

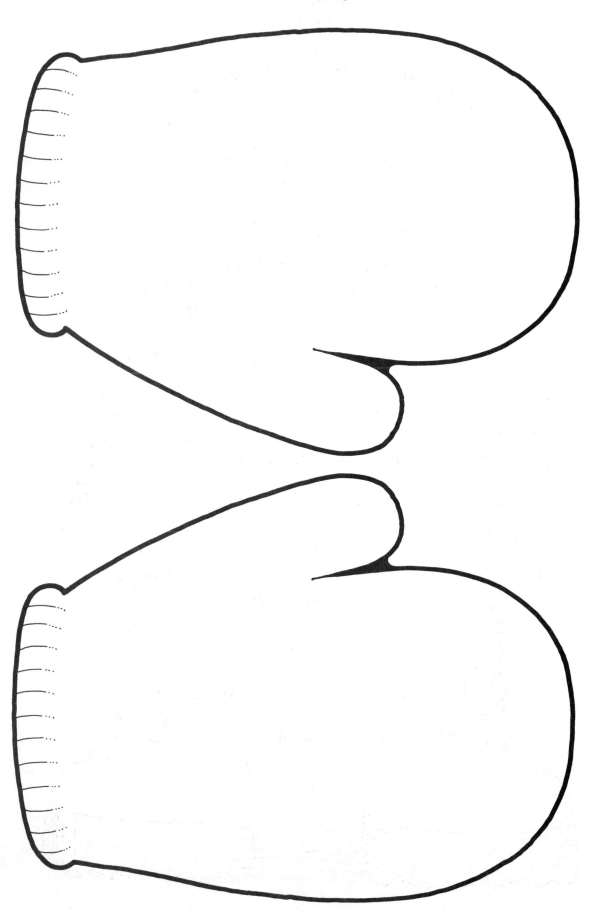

# January

## Space and Exploration

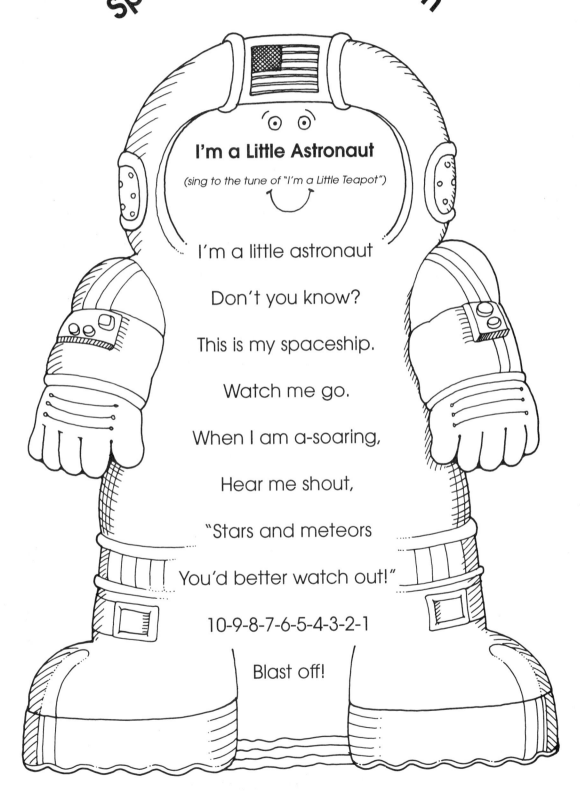

**I'm a Little Astronaut**

*(sing to the tune of "I'm a Little Teapot")*

I'm a little astronaut

Don't you know?

This is my spaceship.

Watch me go.

When I am a-soaring,

Hear me shout,

"Stars and meteors

You'd better watch out!"

10-9-8-7-6-5-4-3-2-1

Blast off!

## Spaceship Launch

**ABC** This game is played like Hangman. Divide the class into small groups, and give each group a Spaceship reproducible. Have one student in each group select a vocabulary word, draw lines to show how many letters are in the word, and give its definition. Invite other students in the group to guess the letters of the word. For each incorrect letter guessed, have the first student color a part of the spaceship on the reproducible. Challenge students to try to finish spelling the word before the spaceship is "launched."

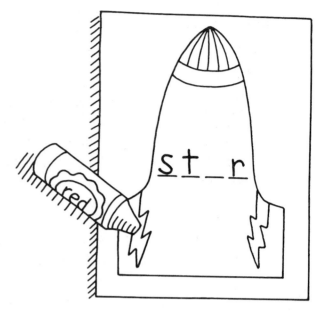

## Story Starters

Attach stickers or space-related pictures to separate index cards, and write a brief sentence relating to each picture. For example, you could write *The astronaut floats* or *I'm going to the Moon* under a picture of an astronaut. Under a picture of a spaceship you could write *3-2-1 Blastoff!* Show each card, and read the sentence to students. Have students copy the sentence in a journal, paying attention to the spaces between the words, and then write a response to it. Tell them they may write their response any way they want. Then, have them illustrate it. Have them read their response to you as you write the interpretation beneath it (if necessary). As students progress, have them write a two-sentence response.

## 3-2-1 Blastoff!

### MATERIALS

Spaceship reproducible
(page 187)

Astronaut reproducible
(page 188)

chart paper (optional)

large construction paper

scissors

glue

crayons or markers

hole punch

class photos

tape

yarn

Invite students to brainstorm space-related words, such as *shooting stars, planets,* and *aliens.* Record their responses on chart paper or the chalkboard. Give each student a Spaceship reproducible and a large sheet of construction paper. Invite students to fold the construction paper into four sections to make an accordion-style book. Ask students to cut out the space-ship pattern, glue it to the top of the folded paper, and then cut around the pattern through all the sheets. Have students color their spaceship and title the cover *Come into My Spaceship.* Have students write or dictate a story using the sentence frames below on each page of their book. (To encourage students to practice the word *we, will,* or *see,* type the sentence frames below, but leave a space for each letter in the word, or words, you want students to practice writing.) Encourage students to use the words they brainstormed earlier to help them complete the frames. Ask students to illustrate each page. Invite each student to color the Astronaut reproducible, cut it out, and attach a student photo to the astronaut's helmet. Have students tape one end of yarn to the back of the astronaut and tape the other end to the bottom inside cover of the book. Encourage students to have the astronaut become part of the spaceship flight as they read their book.

*We are going to _____.*
*We will see _____.*
*We will see _____.*
*We will see _____.*

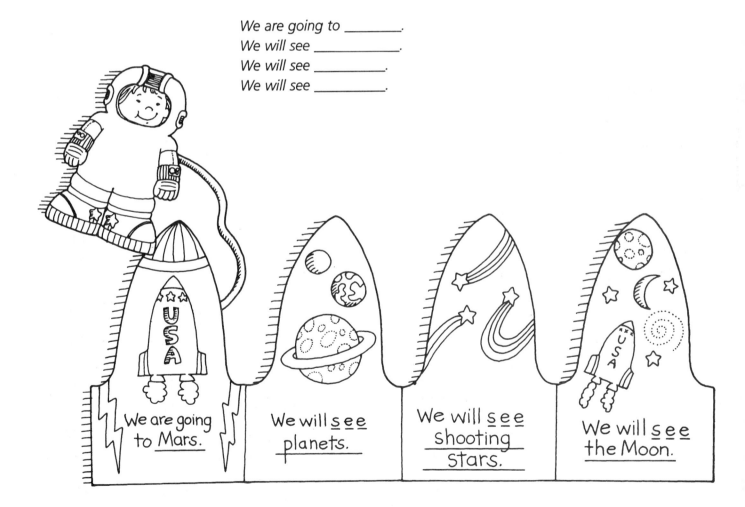

## Mystery Object

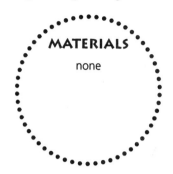

**MATERIALS**

Have students take turns describing an object in detail without identifying the object. They can tell what it is used for and by whom, where it might be found, and what it does. Prompt them to refer to the five senses where appropriate. Invite the class to guess the object's identity after five clues are given.

It is furry and has whiskers. It has a tail. It barks.

## New Discovery

**MATERIALS**

old pillowcase
small objects

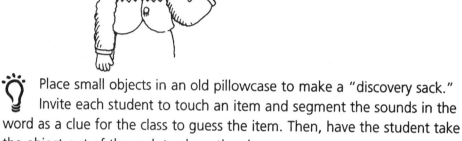
Place small objects in an old pillowcase to make a "discovery sack." Invite each student to touch an item and segment the sounds in the word as a clue for the class to guess the item. Then, have the student take the object out of the sack to show the class.

b-a-t

## Take Me to My Spaceship

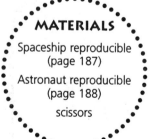

**MATERIALS**

Spaceship reproducible
(page 187)

Astronaut reproducible
(page 188)

scissors

**123** Make an even number of copies of the Spaceship and Astronaut reproducibles, and cut them out. Write a numeral on each astronaut. Draw a quantity of dots on each spaceship that coordinates with the numeral written on each astronaut. Invite students to match each astronaut with its corresponding spaceship.

# Spaceship

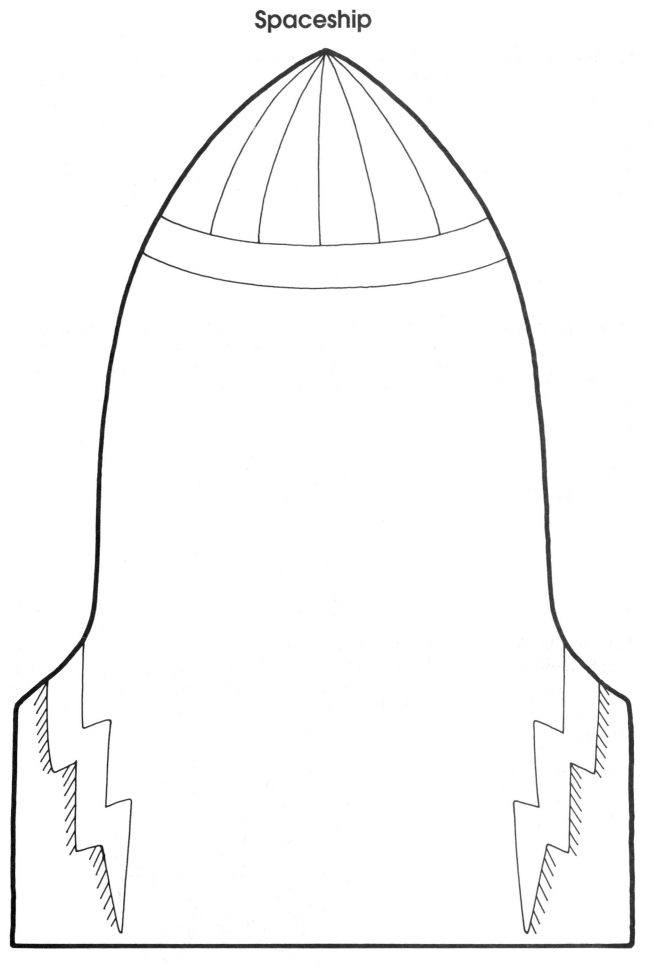

# Astronaut

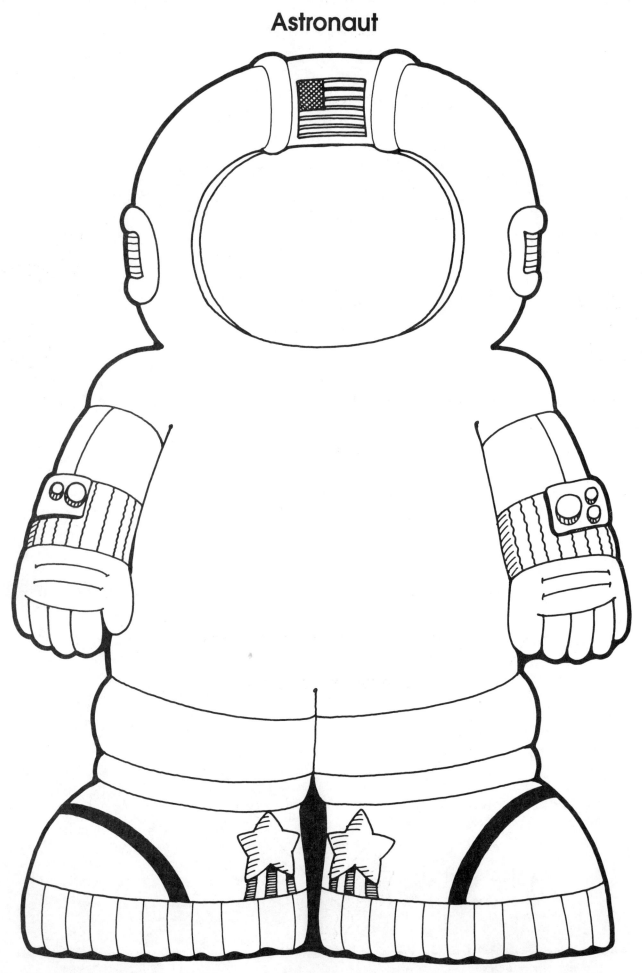

# February

# Hearts and Love

## Valentine

*(sing to the tune of "Jingle Bells")*

Valentine, valentine, have a happy day.

We think you are wonderful

In each and every way.


Valentine, valentine, we send our love to you.

We hope you have fun today

In everything you do.

## Love Dust

Place "love dust" at the center, and invite students to draw a picture that shows a time that they could have used some love dust to solve a problem. For example, a student could draw or write how love dust would have made his sister feel better if she lost her favorite doll.

*I would use love dust to make my mom feel better after a hard day at work.*

## The Kissing Hand

After reading aloud *The Kissing Hand,* discuss with students that a heart and a kiss are symbols for love. In the story, Chester's mother gives him a secret message on his first day of school by kissing the palm of his hand. Whenever he misses his mother, he places his palm on his cheek to feel her kiss. Invite students to create other symbols to represent positive messages, such as sharing, caring, and listening. Have students use their symbol to write secret messages to their classmatess. After discussing the book, teach students a "secret message" to share—the sign in sign language for *I love you.* At the end of the day, let your "kissing hand" "kiss" the fingers of each student in the room. It is a tender way to say good-bye.

## Friendly Valentine

Give each student a copy of the song below. Have students glue it to an envelope. Invite students to decorate the front of the envelope and write a message to a friend or family member on the back.

 **Friendly Little Valentine**
*(sing to the tune of "The Noble Duke of York")*

Oh, this friendly little valentine
Has come your way to say
You're someone very special.
Have an especially happy day.

## Floating Hearts

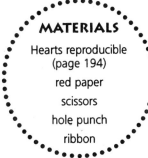

**MATERIALS**

Hearts reproducible
(page 194)

red paper

scissors

hole punch

ribbon

Copy the Hearts reproducible on red paper, and cut out the hearts. Brainstorm with students loving, positive words or phrases, such as *You worked hard, Terrific, I like your idea, Pretty nifty, You're my friend, I'll share with you, I forgive you, Sure, All right, Can I help?, Thank you, Yes!, Good for you, You are kind, Today is a good day, Good try!,* and *I like you.* Write a word or phrase on each heart, punch a hole at the top of each heart, and tie a piece of ribbon to it. Hang the hearts from the ceiling, on a bulletin board, or from a small tree to create a display of floating hearts. Tell students *Love is spoken here.* Choose one heart every day, and read it with the class. Challenge students to use that word or phrase as often as possible throughout the day. Prepare extra hearts to add to the display when students want to add new loving words or phrases. When unloving words are exchanged among students, remind them that love is spoken here, and refer to the words on the floating hearts.

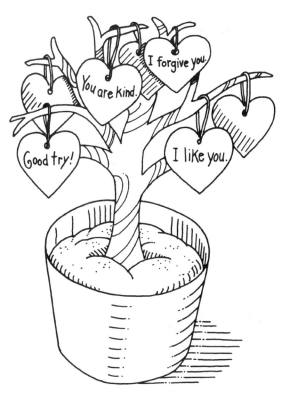

## Concentration

**MATERIALS**

12 heart cutouts

**ABC** In advance, write six capital letters on separate heart cutouts and the matching lowercase letters on the remaining cutouts. Turn the cutouts facedown. Mix them up. Have students take turns turning over one card, then another, trying to find its partner. If a pair is found, have students remove the cards from the table and continue to play. If a pair is not found, the next player takes a turn.

## How Many Hearts Are in the Bag?

•• MATERIALS ••
red or pink butcher paper
scissors
stapler
resealable plastic bag
heart candies
library card pouches
craft sticks

**123** In advance, cut a large heart shape from red or pink butcher paper. Title the heart *How Many Hearts Are in the Bag?* Staple a resealable plastic bag of heart candy on the heart. Label three library card pouches with *Less than 20, Exactly 20,* and *More than 20,* and staple them to the heart. Invite each student to place a craft stick in the appropriate pouch. Have students check their estimate by counting the heart candies.

## Heart Cookies

Slice frozen cookie dough, and give each student a piece. Invite students to form heart shapes by squeezing and poking the dough. After baking, have students frost and decorate the heart-shaped cookies with small candies.

# The Lollipop Tree

## MATERIALS

lollipops
soil
water
radish seeds
chart paper
rulers
student journals
hot glue gun
tree branch

To do this activity for Valentine's Day, begin by February 1st. Begin by telling a story or singing the song about how a "lollipop tree" grew from planting lollipops. Afterwards, give each student a lollipop. Have students prepare the soil near your classroom, plant the lollipop sticks, and water the ground. After the students have left for the day, plant some radish seeds near the sticks. Continue to water near the sticks every day. Ask students to predict whether or not they think the lollipop sticks will grow into a lollipop tree, and use their responses to create a graph. Ask students to make predictions about what they expect will happen to the lollipop sticks. Have students brainstorm ideas about what they could do if a tree really did grow. Ask questions such as *Would a red lollipop stick grow a red lollipop tree? Would one tree grow or many? How big would the tree be? How long would it take for a tree to grow?* As the radish seeds sprout, have students measure them for growth, but do not tell the students what is really growing. Have students record in their journals the changes they see in the garden.

Before students arrive on Valentine's Day, dig up the radishes and plant a lollipop tree. (This requires some preparation on your part.) Use a hot glue gun to fasten a hundred or so lollipops to a tree branch. Carefully transport the branch to school, and plant it without the students seeing you. (You will find as the years pass that students will return to visit you each year in anticipation of the lollipop tree.) You may want to have an extra basket of lollipops handy to share with your many visitors. After the students discover the lollipop tree, retell the story and talk about the exciting news. Direct their thoughts to fact and fantasy. Tell students *Maybe it's real, and maybe it's not, but what IS real is the excitement and fun and love we have together. Whatever is real, and whatever is pretend, lollipop trees will probably only grow in our garden here at school because we have a special kind of magic. If you ever want to share in the magic of our lollipop tree again, all you have to do is come back to visit.* After the lollipops have all been taken from the branch, secretly remove the tree branch after school hours.

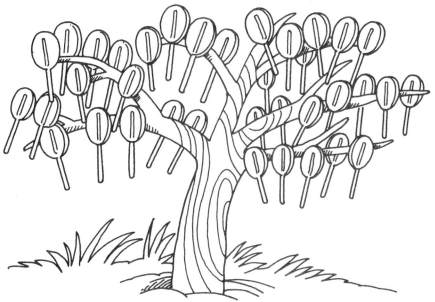

# Hearts

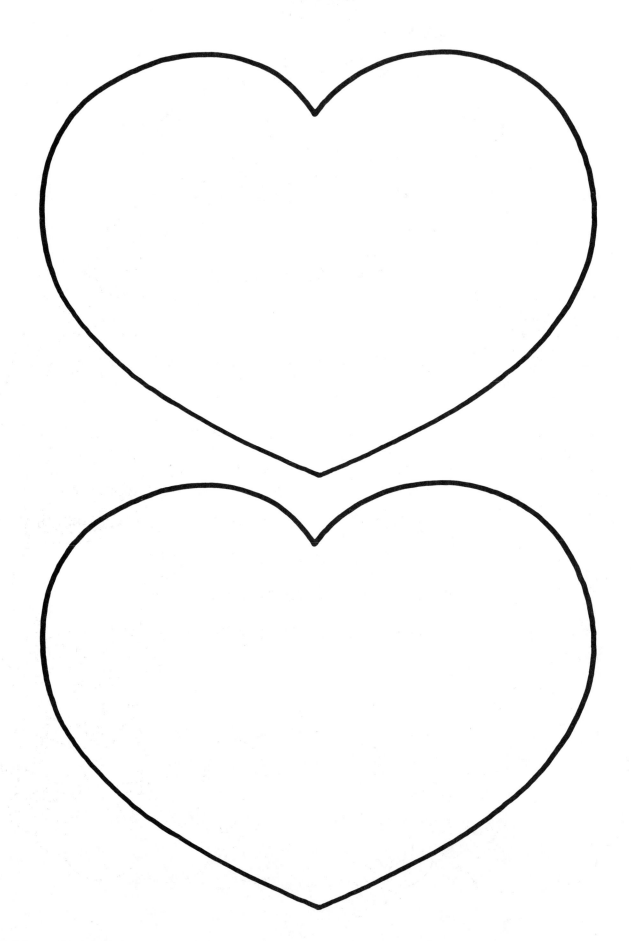

# Shamrocks and Leprechauns

## The Little Leprechaun

*(sing to the tune of "Yankee Doodle")*

There was a little leprechaun

As funny as could be.

I tried and tried to catch him,

But he ran away from me.

So I followed the big rainbow.

I was feeling rather bold,

And at the end I found him.

He gave me his pot of gold.

## Golden Words

### MATERIALS

Coins reproducible
(page 199)

six clean, empty juice cans

red, orange, yellow, green,
blue, purple construction
paper

glue

scissors

**ABC** Glue a different color of construction paper around each of six empty cans. Write on each can a different rime, such as -et, -it, -ig, -at, -all, and -ug. Arrange the cans to make a rainbow. Make several copies of the Coins reproducible. Write on each coin a different onset, such as *b, spl, p, ch, sm,* and *h,* and have students help you cut them out. Give each student a coin cutout. Invite students to identify a rime that will make a word when combined with their onset. For example, a student could place a coin with the onset *pl* in the can marked with the rime *-ug.* When all coins have been placed, have students take turns reading the new words. Invite students to mix the coins again and sort them into the cans to make and read new words.

## Just Our Luck

### MATERIALS

Coins reproducible
(page 199)

butcher paper

scissors

stapler

crayons or colored
pencils

Create a rainbow and pot from butcher paper. Staple the rainbow to a covered board. Attach the pot to one end of the rainbow, and title the board *Just Our Luck.* Encourage students to draw pictures or write about things they feel they are lucky to have or people they are lucky to know on the Coins reproducible. Invite students to attach their "lucky" coins to the pot at the end of the rainbow.

## Blarney Pie

### MATERIALS

chocolate graham crackers
resealable plastic bags
wooden blocks
paper cups
gold-wrapped chocolate coins
green food coloring
vanilla pudding
plastic spoons
whipped cream

Give each student a chocolate graham cracker in a resealable plastic bag. Have students crush their cracker with a wooden block and then pour the crumbs into a paper cup. Have students place a gold-wrapped chocolate coin in their cup. Add green food coloring to vanilla pudding. Invite students to add a spoonful or two of the green pudding and a dollop of whipped cream to their cup. Enjoy Blarney Pie together for a delightful St. Patrick's Day treat.

## Potato People

### MATERIALS

large brown construction paper
scissors
construction-paper scraps
crayons
glue
green heart cutouts

In advance, cut out large potato shapes from brown construction paper. Invite students to use construction-paper scraps and crayons to create "potato people" such as a character from a book or a famous individual. Show students how to make accordion arms or legs to add to their potato person. Invite students to glue three green heart cutouts together to make shamrocks.

# Treasure Hunt

**MATERIALS**

Shamrocks reproducible
(page 200)

green paper

scissors

green footprint cutouts

treats

Copy the Shamrocks reproducible on green paper, write clues such as the ones below on separate shamrocks, and cut them out. Arrange clues around the room so that one clue leads to the next. Place green footprint cutouts between the clues. Place a treat such as gold-wrapped chocolate coins for the class at the last clue. You may want to set the treasure under a rainbow bulletin board to continue the legend. Invite students to follow the clues to find the treasure.

I'm a little leprechaun
As funny as can be.
I've hidden golden coins
But you must look carefully.

I'm not here.
Where did I go?
Check the _____
And soon you'll know!

Put on a smile.
Blink one, two, three.
Look by the _____
And soon you'll see.

Pretty clever,
Don't you think?
Run to the _____
As quick as a wink.

Not here. Not here.
Look high and low.
But check the _____
Before you go.

Good for you, my little friends.
This hunt is coming to an end.
Look under the _____ for your last clue.
It will tell you what to do.

Somewhere there's a rainbow
That's really neat.
If you figure this out
You'll find the treat.

Spring has sprung.
You're a whiz.
This is where the treasure is.
Happy St. Patrick's Day!

Somewhere there's a rainbow
That's really neat.
If you figure this out
You'll find the treat.

# Coins

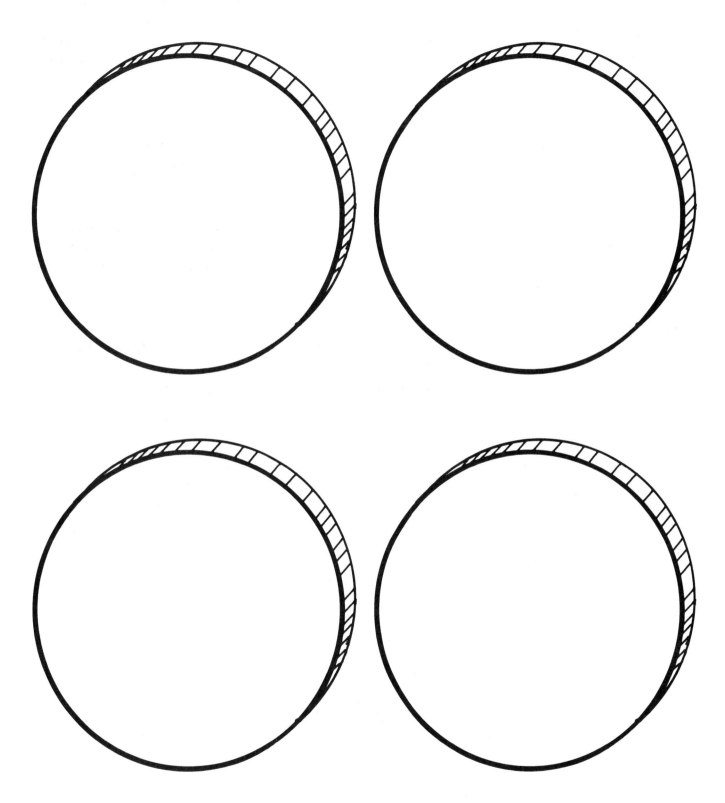

# Shamrocks

# April

## Spring and Animals

**Zigity Zagity Moo**

Zigity zagity moo.

I'm going to the zoo.

A zebra, a seal, an elephant, too.

Lions and tigers and even a gnu.

So pack the car. Let's get on our way.

We're off to the zoo . . .

What a wonderful spring day!

## Flipping Eggs

### MATERIALS

Egg reproducible
(page 205)

scissors

stapler

**ABC** Make seven copies of the Egg reproducible, and cut out the eggs. Cut six of the eggs in half. Take six halves, and arrange them into a stack. (You will use the other six halves to create another flip book.) Staple the six halves on the left side of the seventh whole egg. Write a different onset (e.g., *b, c, f, h, m, p*) on each egg half. Write a rime (e.g., *-at*) to the right of the stack on the bottom egg. Show students how to flip the pages to create new words. Use the other six egg halves and another whole egg cutout to create a flip book with a different set of onsets and rime.

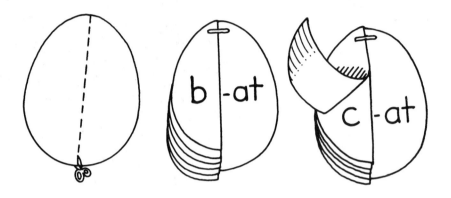

## What's in the Egg?

### MATERIALS

Egg reproducible
(page 205)

scissors

construction paper

crayons or markers

bookbinding
materials

Make five copies of the Egg reproducible, and copy each of the sentence frames below on a separate page. Photocopy a set of revised pages for each student. Have students cut out the shapes, cut an egg-shaped construction-paper cover, and title it *What's inside the Egg?* Invite students to complete the sentence frames and illustrate the pages. Bind the pages together into individual books.

*Maybe it's a _____.*
*Maybe it's a _____.*
*I wish it were a _____.*
*I hope it's not a _____.*
*Look! It's a _____. What a surprise!*

## Pass the Basket

**MATERIALS**

small slips of paper
plastic eggs
basket
music on cassette/CD
cassette/CD player

Write different numerals or equations on small slips of paper, and put each in a separate plastic egg, one per student. Place the eggs in a basket. Invite students to sit in a circle. Play music while students pass the egg basket. When the music stops, have the student who is holding the basket select an egg. Tell the student to read the number or solve the equation on the slip of paper and clap that number of times. Start the music again, and continue the game until each egg has been opened.

## At the Zoo

**MATERIALS**

drawing paper
crayons or markers
glue
construction paper
bookbinding materials

In advance, type the sentence frames below and make one copy for each student. Have students verbally complete the following sentence frames:

*At the zoo, the (describing word   animal name) (action animal does).*
*I like the (describing word   animal), but the (describing word   animal) is kind of _____.*

For example, students might say *At the zoo, the silly monkey swings from a tree. I like the huge hippo, but the growling lion is kind of scary.* Record each student's responses in the blanks. Invite students to illustrate their story and glue it to a construction-paper background. Ask students to act out their story. Invite classmates to guess the identity of the zoo animals. Bind the pages together for a class book

## Animal Roundup

### MATERIALS

Farm Animals Picture
Cards (page 206)

crayons or colored pencils

scissors

**123** Have students work in small groups. Give each student a copy of the Farm Animals Picture Cards to color and cut out. Ask each student in the group to combine his or her cards into one pile. Invite students to categorize the animals. Students might group the animals according to their color, size, number of legs, etc.

## Riddles

### MATERIALS

Farm Animals Picture
Cards (page 206)

crayons or markers

scissors

Have students work in pairs or small groups. Give each pair or small group a copy of the Farm Animals Picture Cards to color and cut out. Have students place the cards facedown in a pile. Have each student draw a card from the pile and create three clues about the animal. Students guess what they think the answer could be. Allow three or four responses for each clue. For example, a student might say *I am fluffy. I am small. Sometimes I am yellow. I hatched from an egg. What am I?* (a chick)

# Egg

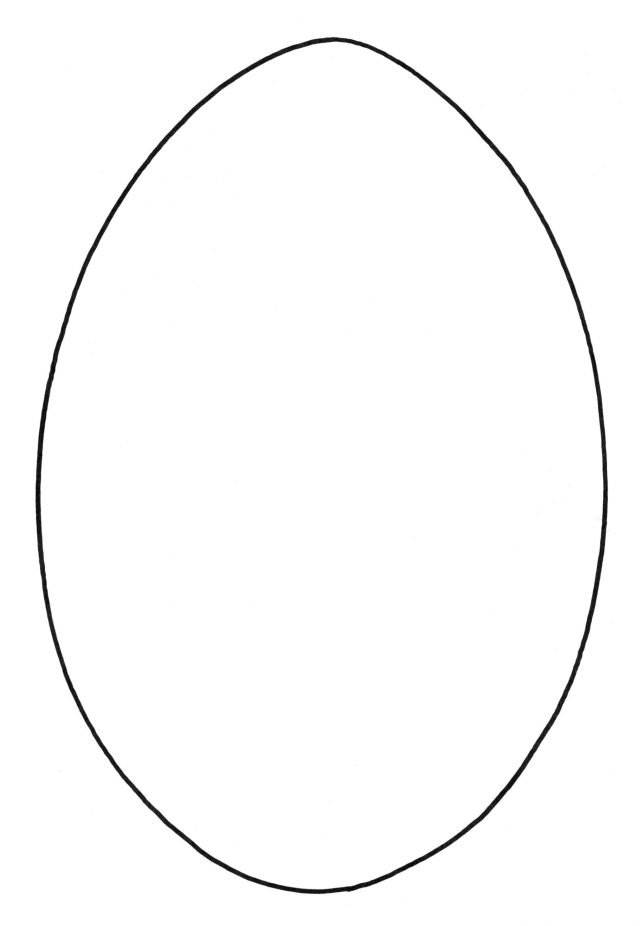

# Farm Animals Picture Cards

May

# Family

**My Family**

This is my family.

It's filled with love.

We fit together

Like a hand in a glove.

We laugh. We play.

We work. We share.

We know many ways

To show that we care.

*(Have students list ways they show they care.)*

## All in the Family

**123** Use a copy of each student's class photo to graph on chart paper the number of siblings in the student's family. Invite students to copy this graph on the Graph reproducible. Have students label and number their graph and color the number of boxes for each number of siblings that coordinates with the information on the graph.

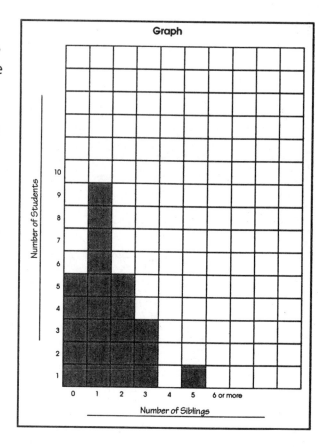

## Family Fun

Have each student fold a piece of newsprint into four sections and write one of the following words in each quadrant: *Beginning, Middle, Middle, End.* Encourage students to tell a story about something their family has done or likes to do together. Record their words, as dictated, at the bottom of each section. Invite students to illustrate their story in sequence from beginning to end.

## I Love My Mother Because . . .

**MATERIALS**

black markers
drawing paper
bookbinding materials

Have each student use a black marker to draw an outline of his or her mother, or special friend, on drawing paper. Then, invite students to complete the sentence frame *I love my mother because* _____. Write *The most important thing about my mom is that she loves me* on two separate sheets of paper. Place one of the sheets at the beginning of the book as a title page and the other at the end of the book. Photocopy the pages and compile them to make a book for each student. Add a cover with the title *Loving Our Mothers*. Give students a copy of the book to share with their mother at a Mother's Day party to be hosted by the students (see page 210).

## Mother's Day Bath Salts

**MATERIALS**

Dear Mom reproducible (page 212)
40-pound (18 kg) bag of water-softening salts (less than $5 at hardware stores)
resealable plastic bags
food coloring
scented oil

Have each student scoop two cupfuls of water-softening salts into a resealable plastic bag. (Forty pounds of water-softening salts allows 2 cups of salt per child for a class of 25.) Invite students to add a few drops of food coloring and a few drops of scented oil to their bag. Have students securely seal their bag and squish it around to mix the color and scent. Have students place a copy of the Dear Mom reproducible inside the bag or attach it to the bag for a Mother's Day treat.

## Mother's Day Mother Goose Party

For Mother's Day, have each student come to school dressed as a different character from a nursery rhyme. Dress as Mother Goose (or a male nursery-rhyme character) for the day. Wear a long skirt, a shawl or tablecloth over your shoulders, a floppy hat, and glasses. If you have a stuffed goose, carry it around. Have students write invitations to their mothers and grandmothers or other significant women in their life. Prior to the party, create an awning of bright butcher paper, and fold the flaps back like a circus tent to look like opening doors. Have students recite their own nursery rhyme in front of the class and guests with the awning as a backdrop. Invite students to hold props during their presentation. For example, Jack and Jill could have a bucket, Jack Be Nimble could hold a candlestick, and Jumping Joan could have a jump rope. Set up a desk lamp as a spotlight with aluminum foil around it to shine on the student making a presentation. This makes a great photo opportunity and makes students feel extra special. Have students sing Mother's Day songs, recite poems, and share a story or dictation of why they love their mother.

## Snack Stations

Set up several stations with supplies and simple directions so students can make appropriate Mother Goose snacks with their guest. To make Queen of Hearts Tarts, have students place a spoonful of cream cheese and a spoonful of jam on a graham cracker square. To make Little Miss Muffet Curds and Whey, have students place a spoonful of cottage cheese in a small cup and add a spoonful of pineapple chunks on top. To make Peter, Peter Pumpkin Eater Pumpkin Pie Tarts, have students place a spoonful of pumpkin-flavored instant pudding in a small cup and top with a dab of whipped topping. To make Blackbirds in a Pie, have students use their finger to poke a black jelly bean through a marshmallow.

# Graph

# Dear Mom

Dear Mom,

You are very special
In each and every way.
The many things you always do
Keep you busy night and day.

And so, please use these bath salts
As your day comes to an end
To rest, relax, and ponder,
Your frazzled nerves to mend.

Please know how much I love you.
You are kind in every way.
You make me glad to be alive.
Thanks and Happy Mother's Day!

- - - - - - - - - - - - - - - - - - - - - - - - - - - - - - - - - - - - - - - - - - - - - - - - - - - - - - - - - - - -

Dear Mom,

You are very special
In each and every way.
The many things you always do
Keep you busy night and day.

And so, please use these bath salts
As your day comes to an end
To rest, relax, and ponder,
Your frazzled nerves to mend.

Please know how much I love you.
You are kind in every way.
You make me glad to be alive.
Thanks and Happy Mother's Day!

# Circus

### The Circus

The circus is here!

Hip, hip, hooray!

It's going to be a wonderful day!

Peanuts, popcorn, and a big parade,

Cotton candy and a cold lemonade,

Elephants, horses, and acrobats, too,

They make me happy. How about you?

I like the lions. I like the bears.

Look at the clown. He's juggling chairs.

The man on the trapeze bravely swings through the air

While the chimpanzees play without any care.

The day has been perfect with so much to see.

I'm glad you came to the circus with me.

Circus Peanuts

Ice Cold Lemonade

## Rhyming Clown Hats

### MATERIALS

Rhyming Words Picture Cards (pages 113–115)

12" x 18" (30.5 cm x 46 cm) sheets of construction paper

stapler

crayons or markers

scissors

glue

ABC Help each student roll a large sheet of construction paper into a cone and staple it together to make a clown hat. Have each student sort through a set of the Rhyming Words Picture Cards to find two or more rhyming pictures. Have students read their rhyming words, color them, cut them out, and glue them to their hat. Invite students to wear their hat and practice reading the hats of their classmates. Challenge students to find other students who have pictures that rhyme with their own words.

## The Circus Is Here!

### MATERIALS

Circus Tent reproducible (page 216)

crayons or colored pencils

bookbinding materials

Make a photocopy of the Circus Tent reproducible. Write in the top part of the tent the sentence frame *This is a circus _____*. Make a copy of the revised circus tent for each student. Invite students to complete the sentence frame with a circus word (e.g., clown, elephant, acrobat). Encourage students to illustrate their work. Bind students' pages together into a class book titled *The Circus Is Here!*

## How Many at the Circus?

### MATERIALS

Circus Tent reproducible
(page 216)

crayons or markers

**123** Give each student a Circus Tent reproducible. Assign each student a number to write in the top part of the tent. Invite students to choose one person or thing related to the circus, and have them use the number at the top of their tent to determine how many people or things to draw. For example, a student with the number six could draw six clowns or six sticks of cotton candy. Post student work on a board titled *How Many at the Circus?*

## All Aboard!

### MATERIALS

Train reproducible
(page 217)

paper

scissors

glue

When taking dictation for a class story, write or type each sentence on paper. Have each student cut out his or her sentence and glue it to a copy of the Train reproducible. Invite a student to glue the title of the story on the engine and a concluding sentence on the caboose. Invite students to arrange and rearrange each car to tell the story in a different sequence. Keep the story at a center for independent activities.

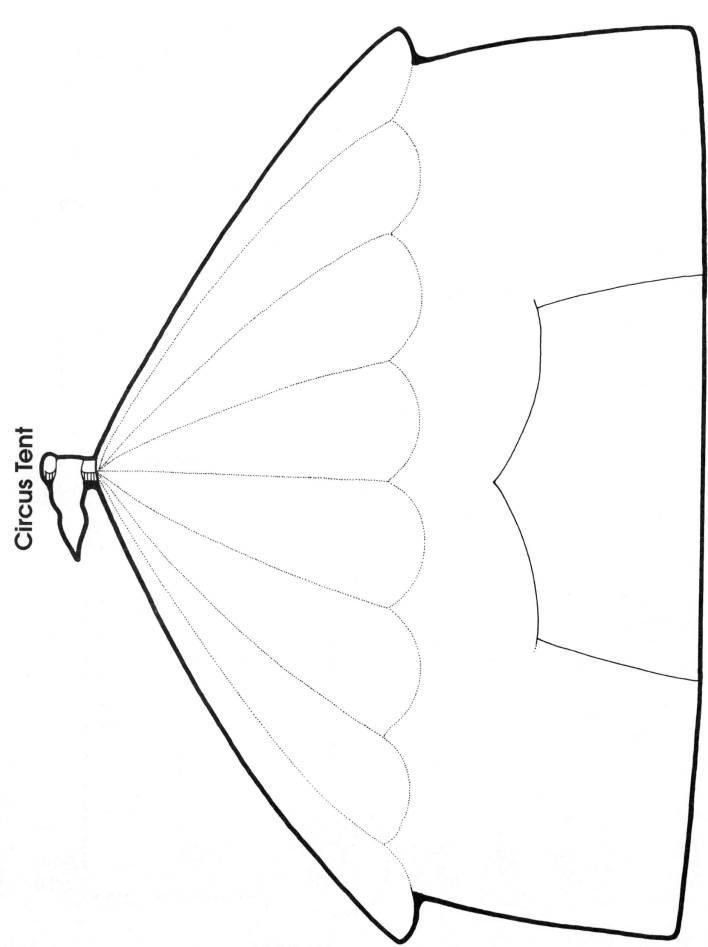

Circus Tent

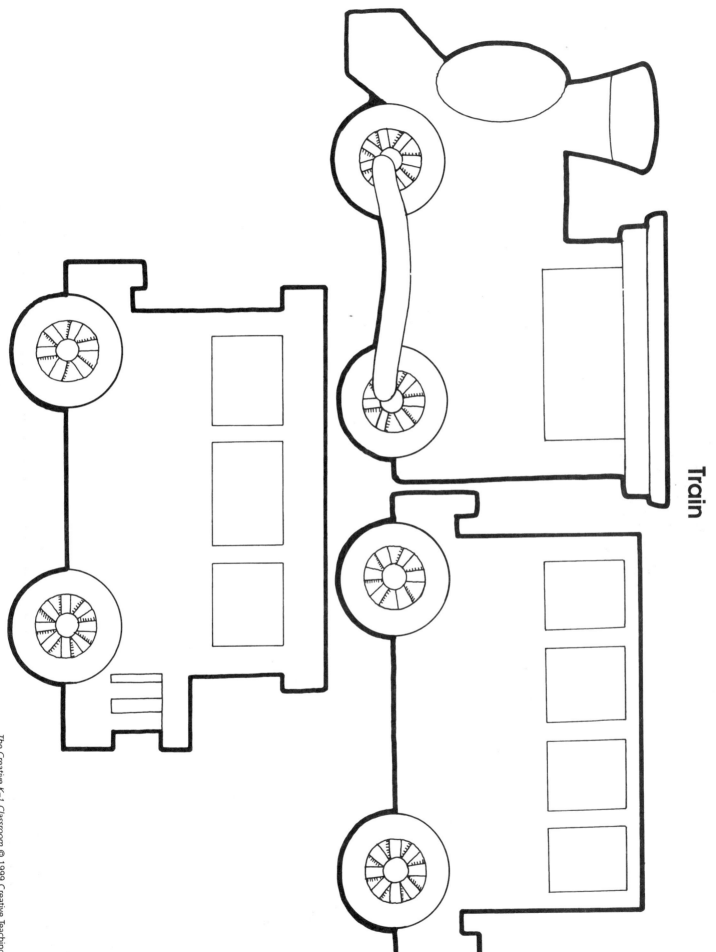

Train

# MAKING MEMORIES

Give your students something concrete to look

back on, something that will bring to mind the many exciting

times in your year together. Select one of the following ideas to devel-

op throughout the year. At the conclusion of the year, present a

memory book to each student. There is no greater gift

than happy memories.

## The Year in Review

### MATERIALS
colored construction paper
bookbinding materials
photos of class events
tape or glue

At the beginning of the year, bind a blank book from sheets of colored construction paper. As you develop photographs, add them to the book. Encourage students to write captions for each picture. Store the book at the Literacy Center for independent-reading time.

## Class Memory Book

**MATERIALS**

student artwork, poetry,
and writing

colored construction
paper

Collect student samples of artwork, poetry, and writing that represent each month of the year. Mount the work on pieces of colored construction paper. Use the following ideas as a guideline for each month:

### September

- Take a photograph of each student during the first week of school. Save the photos to use on the cover of the memory book at the end of the year.
- Send home an assignment the first week of school where each student, with the help of parents, selects four goals he or she would like to achieve during the school year. Have students illustrate their work and return it to class.
- Have students use orange, red, yellow, and brown crayons to make rubbings of leaves. Have students sponge over their rubbing with blue food coloring that has been diluted with water.

### October

- Have students use a white crayon to draw a picture about Halloween. Invite students to paint over their picture with black watercolor and then add a favorite Halloween poem.

### November

- Have students make a list of things they are thankful for and illustrate it.
- Add photos of the students dressed like Pilgrims.

### December

- Send home an assignment to write about holiday traditions. Have students illustrate their work.
- Attach a photo of the school holiday program or a visit from Santa.

### January

- Have students make a list of New Year's resolutions and illustrate their list.

### February

- Have students make a winter picture that includes snowmen and snowflakes.
- Invite students to write a story about being a hero.
- Include a photo of the students dressed up as George Washington or Abraham Lincoln.

**March**

- Have students use watercolor paints to make a rainbow on wet paper. When the papers dry, use a black permanent marker to record on the painted paper a poem or story dictated by each student.

**April**

- Invite students to sprinkle powdered tempera paint on a piece of white paper, place the paper on cookie sheets, and take it outside in the rain.
- Fill a small coffee can with water. Add dish soap, and use a straw to blow bubbles in the soapy water. Squirt yellow, green, and blue food coloring on top of the bubbles. Have students press a piece of paper over the top and blow some more bubbles. Add some more food coloring, and have students press the paper again. Have students press the paper to the bubbles three times.

**May**

- Invite students to use a black permanent marker to outline a vase shape with flowers. Have students moisten their paper with a spray bottle and use pastel watercolors to make splashes of color.

**June**

- Take a photograph of each student to include on the cover of a memory book. Design the cover to have two flowers, one short and one tall. In the center of the short flower, put the student's beginning-of-the-year photo. In the tall flower, put the end-of-the-year photo. Add the following caption:

  *Me, oh my, but time has flown.*
  *Just look, my friends, at how I've grown.*

- Have students write about the things they learned in class during the year and the happy memories they have made. Have them include an illustration.

Other pages might include the following:

- Have students take turns saying nice things about each of their classmates. Record these comments on separate pages for each student.
- Attach a large envelope or pouch to a page or the back cover to hold samples of student writing throughout the year.
- Make a montage of photographs taken throughout the year. Be certain to include a class photo.
- Include a class theme song or favorite poem.

## Classroom Cookbook

### MATERIALS
drawing paper
black markers
bookbinding materials

If cooking is a regular part of your program, be certain to have students dictate or write the recipes (as nearly as they can recollect). Or, invite students to write or dictate their favorite recipes from home. Have them use a black permanent marker to illustrate each recipe. Duplicate each recipe so each student has a copy of the Classroom Cookbook.

## Portfolio

### MATERIALS
student work samples
file folders

Collect samples of student work throughout the year as a form of authentic assessment. Have students create the same sample at the middle and the end of the year to show student progress. Write the date on each piece. Label file folders with each student's name, and file the work samples throughout the year. Place the portfolio pieces in a memory book for each student at the end of the year. Include items such as the following:

- self-portrait
- monthly writing sample
- numbers and letters
- spelling words
- stories
- drawings

## Class Coloring Book

### MATERIALS
drawing paper
black permanent marker
construction paper
bookbinding materials

Capture the memories of the year in a coloring book that each student takes home at the end of the year. For each special event, have a student dictate a few remarks and make an outline drawing of the activity with a black permanent marker. Be certain the student signs his or her name. Collect the pages during the year. As the year draws to a close, photocopy the pages, and bind each set of pages with a construction-paper cover into a special coloring book for each student to take home and treasure. A sentimental cover letter by you will make it a lasting treasure. Use the following example as a model:

Dear Friend,

It's hard to believe that the year is over. I've grown to love you SO much. Please remember there's nothing you can't do if you just try. I'll be keeping my eye out for you over the years, and I'll be anxious to see the wonderful person you become.

I hope you'll keep this coloring book as a happy reminder of the wonderful memories we made together. Also, if you will practice reading it each day this summer, it will give you a great start for next year. Enjoy it, and think of me.

I love you.

## Alphabet Anthology

**MATERIALS**

student poems, artwork, and writing
file folders
bookbinding materials

Throughout the year, make an anthology of favorite poems, student artwork, and writing samples representing the letters of the alphabet. File the papers sequentially, one folder for each child. At the end of the year, bind each student's papers into one book for a perfect way to preserve the precious memories of the year. The following is a list of suggestions for each letter.

A—apple art, ants, acorns
B—bus, bubble painting, butterflies
C—cowboys, circus, caterpillars
D—ducks, Dad, dimes
E—eggs, emotions, elephants
F—frogs, friends, families
G—goldfish, grandparents, groundhogs
H—homes, Hawaii, hands
I—ice cream, inches, inventions
J—jack-o-lantern, jungle, jelly beans
K—kangaroo, kindness, kaleidoscope
L—ladybugs, leprechaun, Lincoln
M—Marvelous Me, Mom, manners
N—noodles, names, nursery rhymes
O—ocean, octopus, Olympics
P—popcorn, puppets, pigs
Q—Queen of Hearts, quilts, quarters
R—rainbow, rocks, rain
S—spiders, snowflakes, stars, spring
T—turkey, teddy bear, turtle, twins
U—Uncle Sam, ugly bugs, unicorns
V—valentines, volcanoes, vegetables
W—Washington, worms, wishes
X—kisses (i.e., X's and O's), x-rays
Y—yak, yo-yo, yellow submarine
Z—zoo, zero, zigzag

Write the following poem on the cover:

*Kindergarten (or first grade) is a happy place.*
*There is always a smile on everyone's face.*
*With everything we learn and do,*
*Each day's an adventure that starts anew.*

# PULLING IT ALL TOGETHER

So how do you make all of this work and still have
a life of your own?

It all begins with getting organized. Determine what is important and schedule
it on your yearly calendar before the year begins. Then, stick to your schedule. Teach
explicitly to your goals in a sequential and systematic manner and you will use your time
more efficiently and effectively.

Make certain your students are constantly engaged in worthwhile activities. When they are done with
one activity do they know what to do next without asking you?

Make appropriate behavior the standard and do not settle for anything less. Precious time is wasted
when you have to punish, negotiate, cajole, beg, plead, answer a litany of questions, and reward every
little good deed. Teach the students to make good decisions, solve their own problems, and answer
their own questions. Provide them with a curriculum that is exciting and suited to their needs and
they will much rather be a part of the group than be isolated for inappropriate behavior.

Practice Prescriptive Teaching. You cannot possibly meet the needs of each student in your
class unless you know where each one is. Assess and monitor students' growth on a
regular basis so you can genuinely Teach to Reach Each. Create windows of
time to teach one-on-one and in small groups by providing the rest of
the class with meaningful opportunities to learn and
explore without your direct supervision.

Simplify. Eliminate the things that really do not matter. If you are feeling rushed, then it is time for something to go. Do not spend time tracing patterns. Let the students learn how to create their own materials. Do you really have to do everything you have planned? It is not how much you accomplish in a day that matters. It is what the students have learned and how they feel about the day's activities that is important. If the students feel rushed, the quality of their work will suffer and they will feel irritable and quarrelsome. Simplify. Make your room a joyful place to be.

Planning, organizing, and implementing a playful learning environment is of significant importance in helping you maximize the learning of your students. Teaching the students to act responsibly and to make good decisions on their own will free you to meet the special needs of each student in your care.

And remember—just as learning should be playful, so should teaching. Your own effectiveness as a teacher depends greatly on the joy you find in your work.

Here are some final words of encouragement as you design your own creative K–1 classroom:

*Look for the wonders in each new day.*
*Look to the students to brighten your way.*
*Take time to tend to the needs of each one,*
*But don't forget some time for fun.*

*Take time to listen, to laugh, and to share.*
*Take time to show just how much you care.*
*For you'll find, when all is said and done,*
*They've learned the most whose hearts you've won.*

| If something is hard, | *Whatever the skill or concept you try,* |
|---|---|
| Then this please do . . . | *First teach,* |
| Teach it early | *Then model,* |
| And follow up with review. | *Then practice,* |
|  | *Then apply.* |